# NONGRADING

## in the

## Elementary School

JOHN L. TEWKSBURY

*The Ohio State University*

CHARLES E. MERRILL BOOKS, INC.

Columbus, Ohio

## MERRILL'S
## INTERNATIONAL EDUCATION SERIES

### Under the Editorship of

**Kimball Wiles**

*Dean of the College of Education*

*University of Florida*

*Library of Congress Catalog Card Number: 67-15145*

PRINTED IN THE UNITED STATES OF AMERICA

# PREFACE

The principal focus of this book is to explain in a simplified manner what nongrading is and how it might work in the elementary school. The presentation deals with certain practical questions that teachers and administrators have about the operation of a nongraded program. Specific examples of different aspects of nongraded programs are included because many teachers and administrators want help in translating ideas from the realm of theory to the level of daily practice. It is one thing to consider the general theory of nongrading and to conclude that the approach seems desirable. It is something else again to understand what nongrading might involve in terms of the specifics of daily school operation. Hopefully, a consideration of these specifics will help teachers and administrators understand more clearly some of the procedures and attendant problems that are likely to be involved in operating a nongraded program.

Among the examples developed for this book are diagrams which illustrate how children might progress from teacher to teacher during their years in a nongraded elementary school. An important feature of the book is that these principal ways of assignment are discussed together so that the reader has the opportunity to compare them. Another feature is the example of a report form for a nongraded school.

The examples of various aspects of nongrading which appear in the following chapters were developed to fit with the usual curriculum found in most elementary schools today — a curriculum that is more subject-centered and pre-planned than it is child-centered, integrated, and emergent. There are a number of good reasons, of course, why the latter type of program might be more desirable; but I feel that in the typical public school, the pre-planned, subject-centered program is likely to continue as the dominant pattern for some time to come. With this in mind, the examples presented here have been designed to fit with such a program.

Nongrading is a way of working with children which a school staff would probably adopt gradually, rather than implement in one dramatic reorganization. In the process of gradual change, definite modifications would need to be effected in the way the curriculum was organized and in the way instruction was conducted. Hopefully, the staff might also consider revisions in the actual *content* of the curriculum. However, the suggestions for a nongraded program presented in this book are not dependent upon extensive modifications in the content of the curriculum.

iii

*To my wife, Joyce*

# TABLE OF CONTENTS

vi

# 1

# The Meaning of Nongrading

## Introduction

In recent years the nongraded elementary school has created considerable interest among persons in education. Teachers and administrators in many school systems indicate a desire to know more about this approach to teaching. They are curious about it, and one of the first questions that is often asked is simply, "What is it? — what is nongrading?" Since this question is so basic, it seems appropriate to begin by considering the meaning of this term.

A helpful way to build an understanding of this new approach is to compare it with a graded school program. In making a comparison, graded and nongraded programs will be viewed as though they were at opposite ends of a continuum. When the essential features of each are examined, it is clear that in theory the plans are opposites. In their actual operation in specific schools, however, we do not find the differences nearly so clear-cut. Usually a compromise has been made between the two plans, and the result is a program that lies somewhere along the continuum rather than at one end or the other. There are few, if any, schools that adhere to a graded program in its fullest extent, and it would be difficult indeed to conduct a program that was one hundred per cent nongraded. Nevertheless, in attempting to build an

1

understanding of nongrading, it is helpful to compare it with the graded plan, and to consider the two as opposites.

## The Graded School

What are the essential features of a graded school? As indicated in the previous paragraph, the description which follows portrays a program that is one hundred per cent graded. In such a program the total work of the elementary school is divided into six levels, more commonly referred to as grades. The work to be accomplished in each grade is clearly designated. It usually consists of specific skills, topics, and textbooks to be covered. All of the boys and girls in a given grade are expected to do only the work reserved for that grade and complete it in a year's time. If they do not complete it, they are retained for a year to repeat all of the work.

Pupils are not helped to progress beyond the designated work for the grade because they are not expected to do this until the following year when they are in the next higher grade. If pupils were permitted to go beyond the designated work, this would interfere with the program conducted by the teacher in the next higher grade.

Similarly, a pupil would not be given work equivalent to that of a lower grade because each child in the grade is expected to do that which is specified for the grade. If he cannot, he does not belong there and should have been retained in a lower grade where the program is at his level.

Many of us who have been teachers realize, of course, the folly of expecting that all children in a given grade should do only the work of that grade. Some of the children are capable of a more challenging program; others would find their school efforts more successful if they could progress more slowly and deal with less complicated materials. The theory of the graded school, however, ignores these realities.

As indicated earlier, there are few, if any, elementary schools in which the graded plan is implemented to its fullest extent. In most so-called graded schools of today, the plan has been modified somewhat; thus it is not at the extreme end of the continuum but more toward the nongraded side. The extent of the movement toward the opposite side depends on the modifications that have been made. Good teachers have always tried to make some adaptations in their instructional program for children of different ability, but if the graded approach really prevails in the school system where the teacher is employed, he is limited in the adaptations he can make. He is expected to give failing marks to the children who cannot do grade-level work, despite the progress they may have made at their own level.

## The Nongraded School

In a nongraded school, the program is not divided into six grades and presented so that children at any given grade are limited to just the work designated for their grade. There is no such thing as second-grade work or fourth-grade work which constitutes a uniform program of instruction that all children in a given classroom must accomplish in a year's time. Instead, an attempt is made to help each child work at the level where he is in each subject, and progress in the best way he can. This is the essence of the nongraded program.

If one pupil in a class is ready to study more advanced skills, he is helped to do so even if this work in a graded school had previously been reserved for the next higher grade. If another pupil in the same classroom needs to devote his efforts to less complicated tasks in reading or arithmetic, he is helped to do so even if this means working on skills which were in the domain of a lower grade in a graded school.

In a nongraded classroom, some children will be studying more advanced materials while others devote their energies to different materials. It is also probable that a given pupil will progress more rapidly in one skill subject than in another. The range of performance in such subjects as reading and arithmetic is likely to extend over many grade levels, unless the children have been assigned to teachers on the basis of performance levels, in which case the range would be somewhat less. The teacher does not expect that all the children will become proficient in the same skills by the end of the year or that all will have completed the same textbooks.

The foregoing explanation of a nongraded program pertains especially to the skill subjects. Work in the content subjects might be handled the same way. However, if it was conducted so that all of the children in a classroom studied the same social studies or science topic at the same time, it would still be possible to practice a nongraded approach. The teacher would simply expect that some children would be able to study the topic in greater depth than others, and would provide for these differences.

In a nongraded program, expectations differ for different children. It is accepted that some will do more than others; the teacher attempts to help each child work at the level where he is and then, through instruction that is adjusted so that he will have reasonable success, to progress as best he can. When a child is eventually assigned to another classroom, he would be helped to do work for which he is ready. The teacher in that class would not expect all children to be up to a certain level when they enter his room. He knows that some pupils will have progressed well into the skills that in a graded school would have been reserved for his grade.

In a nongraded school, boys and girls who are progressing especially slowly may need to spend more than the usual amount of time in the program. Those who take an extra year or two are not "failed," no do they "repeat" work in the skill subjects. They simply continue to study these subjects each year from the points where they left off the previous year. The extra year or two provides additional time to acquire important learnings. It should not be anticipated, however, that the extra time will enable all of these students to catch up with their age mates. Some may, but others may not. The nongraded program will not eliminate the fact that some students perform on a lower level in certain areas of work, but it will give these pupils more of an opportunity to have successful learning experiences at their own level. Illustrations of how a child might move through a nongraded program, including ways he might take an extra year, are provided in Chapter Five.

In actual practice there are few, if any, schools that are completely nongraded. Teachers have generally found it too difficult to vary instruction in each subject for each of twenty-five to thirty-five children in a class. Because of this, compromises are usually made, and the result is a cross between graded and nongraded plans. The work may be more nongraded in some subjects than others, and for some students than others. Certain pupils may be able to work independently at their own levels part of the time, but some may not be able to work as well this way because they lack sufficient maturity. The teacher may keep these children together for sub-group instruction. Although sub-group instruction may not result in work that is adjusted exactly to each child's level of achievement, the work will probably be more appropriate than if everyone in the class was given the same instruction.

Although it is difficult to develop a program that is completely nongraded, this does not have to be interpreted to mean that all efforts to un-grade should be abandoned. Many educators would argue that a little nongrading is more desirable than none at all.

In the comparison of graded and nongraded programs that is being made here, it is important to recall that it is the theoretical differences between the two plans that are being described. These differences are clear-cut. In actual practice, however, there are few schools in which one plan or the other is employed exclusively; we would be apt to find a mixture of the two. The typical graded school of today is not fully graded; it embodies some nongraded practices. Likewise, schools which are said to be nongraded, are unlikely to be completely this way; they contain certain vestiges of graded operation.

In the typical graded school of today, one of the best examples of the partial incorporation of nongraded thinking is the practice of sub-group instruction in reading. This is a fairly common practice in many so-called graded schools, yet it is clearly a move away from the graded side of the continuum toward the nongraded side. By organizing two or three reading groups in his class, the teacher is attempting to adjust instruction in order to work with the children more nearly at the levels where they are. Of course, if the teacher does not allow the top group to progress into reading material that is above grade level, his acceptance of the nongraded approach would be minimal; and the same would be true if he insisted on taking the slower groups through the books for his grade whether or not the pupils were ready.

## Assigning Children to Teachers in Nongraded Schools

In a program that is nongraded, an attempt is made to help each child work at the level where he is in each subject and progress in the best way he can. There are three principal ways in which a program of this type can be implemented:

(1) By providing multi-level instruction in self-contained, heterogeneous classes. Because of the heterogeneous grouping, there would be a wide range in performance levels among children in any given classroom.

(2) By assigning children to self-contained classes according to performance levels and then providing instruction from one class to the next on different levels of difficulty. This plan is sometimes

referred to as homogeneous grouping, inter-classroom achievement grouping, ability grouping, or a multi-track plan.

(3) By regrouping a large aggregation of children from time to time during the day or week to form clusters, or classes, that work on different levels under the direction of different teachers. This plan could be conducted as either a departmentalized program or one involving team teaching. The third plan differs from the other two in that the children are assigned to work with different teachers instead of doing all of their work with one teacher in a self-contained classroom.

Plans 2 and 3 may or may not result in a thoroughly nongraded program; it would depend on whether an individual teacher worked with the children assigned to him in a whole-class manner or whether he provided multi-level instruction. As used here, the term whole-class manner means that all of the children are expected to do the same work in approximately the same time. The term multi-level instruction means that the teacher provides instruction and teaching materials on several levels of difficulty for the children assigned to him and permits the students to progress at different rates.

Even though an attempt is made in Plans 2 and 3 to form more homogeneous instructional groups, the children assigned to a given teacher would still display a considerable range in performance levels. For the program to be thoroughly nongraded, the teacher would need to provide multi-level instruction. If a teacher in Plans 2 or 3 instructs the children assigned to him in the whole-class lockstep manner, then the overall educational program in the school is only partially nongraded; but it is at least partially nongraded, because some attempt is being made in the total school program to adjust the work for pupils of different levels of achievement. The children in the lower performing classes or clusters are not expected to do the same things those in the higher performing groups are doing.

Hereafter in this book, when the term partially nongraded is used it refers to programs similar to Plans 2 or 3 in which the teacher instructs the children assigned to him in a whole-class, lockstep manner; whereas the term thoroughly nongraded is used to refer to programs in which the teacher provides multi-level instruction for the children assigned to him. The latter could occur in either Plans 1, 2, or 3.

In any one of the three major plans for implementing a nongraded program, it would be possible to have single-age or mixed-age classrooms or instructional groups. In Plan 1, for instance, children of the same chronological age could be assigned to a classroom. On the other hand, children of two, or possibly three, age groups could be placed there, in which case there would be a mixed-age class. The one-room school which was so common years ago, is one illustration of a mixed-age class. The <u>combination</u> or <u>split</u> class used today in some graded schools is another example. In the latter example, the older children usually study the curriculum for the higher grade and the younger pupils study the curriculum for the lower grade. Each age group is restricted to the work of its own grade. However, in mixed-age classrooms where the work is nongraded, the boys and girls are helped to do the work for which they are ready, regardless of age.

Plan 2 could also be conducted with either single-age or mixed age classes. As an example of the former, the more able readers of a given chronological age could be assigned to one classroom, while the other children of that age but of a lower reading achievement would be placed in a different room.* Having been assigned this way, the pupils would remain in these rooms for their work in all of the subjects. Sometimes reading performance is not used as the sole criterion by which to form the classes, and instead a combination of various measures of performance is used.

Another way to assign children to classrooms in Plan 2 — one that would result in mixed-age classes — would be to put into the same room pupils of several ages who are at about the same point in reading achievement. In this arrangement, a typical self-contained class might include a few bright seven-year-olds, a number of eight-year-olds, and a few slow nine-year-olds, all of whom performed at about a third grade level in reading. If this procedure for assigning children to classrooms was used, there would probably be a very wide range of performance in other subjects, such as arithmetic. The teacher would hardly be able to teach arithmetic by the whole-class method. Although the children in the class might be fairly homogeneous in their general level of reading at the time of their assignment, they would probably separate quickly because they differ widely in mental ability. Many of the bright seven-year-olds would progress faster in reading than the slow nine-year-olds.

Plan 3 could also be conducted with either single-age or mixed-age groups. A departmentalized or team teaching arrangement could be organized for a large aggregation of children who were the same

---

*A program of this type is sometimes called a multi-track plan.

age. It would also be possible to include two or three age groups in this aggregation. In the latter case, there would be a good bit of overlap in the performance levels of the children of different ages. Those who were fairly homogeneous could be placed in clusters or classes in a given subject, and could be re-grouped for work in different subjects.

Each of the three plans for implementing a nongraded program has its problems. In Plan 1 where heterogeneous grouping is practiced, the teacher is faced with the formidable task of providing multi-level instruction commensurate with the wide range in the children's performance levels. Because of the difficulties of providing for the wide range of achievement levels in heterogeneous classrooms, some teachers believe that Plan 2, where an attempt is made to group children according to performance levels, would make teaching easier. Supposedly, the children in a classroom would be more alike and thus easier to teach, but grouping this way does not eliminate pupil differences. Children grouped by one criterion, such as reading, will still differ greatly in other areas of the curriculum. Even in reading, the differences are not reduced sufficiently to warrant teaching all the children the same thing at the same time. Adjustments for individual differences would still be desirable, and would have to be made if the program was to be more than just partially nongraded.

Plan 3 poses problems too. If a team arrangement is developed, the two, three, or four teachers in the team will find that it is not an easy task to work together to provide nongraded instruction for a large aggregation of 55, 82, or 110 children. If a departmentalized program is organized, this may lead to a more rigid compartmentalization of learning experiences. Some educators favor the self-contained classroom because they feel it makes it easier to conduct integrative learning experiences.

In a few of the schools that have tried to develop nongraded programs, a given teacher remains with his class, or with the children assigned to him for departmentalized work, for two and sometimes three years. This practice is often referred to as *teacher-cycling*. It is not an integral part of the nongraded approach, although some persons seem to have the notion that it is. It may be coupled with a nongraded program, but it certainly does not have to be. In most nongraded schools employing Plans 1 or 2, the children have a new teacher each year, and he does his best at the outset to determine each child's performance levels. He then attempts to conduct an instructional program which takes into account these differences in performance.

Chapter Five deals more extensively with the different ways children have been assigned to teachers in nongraded schools.

## Grading and Nongrading: A Further Discussion of the Meaning of These Two Terms

In the opinion of some educators, the meanings for the terms *grading* and *nongrading* do not involve differences in methods of teaching or ways of organizing children for instruction; the terms pertain solely to differences in the way a curriculum is organized. These educators believe that grading should mean only that certain curriculum items are to be taught to students during a certain period of time, and that nongrading should mean only that these limitations do not exist. They contend that these differences are purely structural, and that differences in the way teachers work with children or differences in the way pupils are organized for instruction are not involved at all.

In a strict sense, perhaps these terms should have only these limited meanings. However, as grading is practiced, it has tended to foster certain types of teaching procedures. For a nongraded program to be put into operation, it is necessary that different teaching procedures be used or that children be organized differently for instruction. Thus to think of grading and nongrading solely in terms of curriculum organization, and entirely apart from these other procedures, creates an artificial separation. If nongrading is to mean anything in practice, certain grouping and/or instructional methods will have to be used. In this book nongrading is viewed in a broader context which includes consideration of the ways in which teachers would need to work with children and the ways in which pupils are assigned to teachers for instruction.

The practice of limiting the meaning of grading and nongrading solely to differences in the way the curriculum is organized has been one of the reasons why some of the research studies comparing the relative effectiveness of graded and nongraded programs have yielded meaningless results. In these studies, little attention was paid to the instructional or grouping procedures that were employed. If teachers were free to have children study at any level in the curriculum, it was accepted that a nongraded program existed, whether or not provision was actually made to help pupils work at these different levels. Similarly, in the graded schools which were used for comparison purposes, little attention was given to whether the children were instructed in lockstep fashion or whether the work was individualized within the confines of the graded content. It is not really feasible to determine whether a program is graded or nongraded unless consideration is given to the teaching and grouping procedures which are employed, because it is these procedures which transform nongrading from a mere expression of intent to something that is real and operative.

## Establishing a Nongraded Program: The Need for Administrative Leadership

In studying individual schools that have developed nongraded programs, this author has become increasingly aware of the importance of administrative leadership in effecting changes in instructional procedures. Without active leadership from the principal and support from the central administration, there is little likelihood that a new program can be introduced. Decisions involving school-wide policies related to curriculum and instruction, and decisions involving the acquisition of new materials must be made if a nongraded program is to be established. In the typical school, teachers are not allowed to make these decisions by themselves. The administrative staff and school board make most of the decisions. Given this situation, we should not expect teachers to be the moving force behind the introduction of a nongraded program. Teachers are in the position of having to wait until persons in official leadership capacity are ready to take action.

Too often we hear that the teachers are to blame for the continuance of out-dated instructional practices. However, it would seem that much of the blame rests with the administrative leaders for being willing to accept out-dated practices for so long, and for not exercising sufficient leadership to see that new practices are considered, tried, and supported, not only by verbal encouragement but also financially. In most of the schools with which the author is acquainted where improved educational procedures are being introduced, the moving force can be traced back to strong administrative leadership.

# Summary

In this chapter the basic features of nongrading have been explained. The theory of this plan for organizing instruction is the direct opposite of the theory for organizing instruction in a graded program. If the graded plan was fully implemented, all children in a given grade would be expected to do the same work in a year's time, no more and no less. If a nongraded program was fully implemented, each child in a given classroom would be helped to engage in learning activities for which he was ready. Since the children would differ in what they were ready to do, they would not all be expected to accomplish the same work in a year's time.

In actual practice, there are few if any schools where graded or nongraded programs are fully implemented. Usually we find a combination of the two approaches with a greater emphasis toward one or the other.

It was pointed out that educators differ somewhat in the meaning they attach to the term nongraded. Some of these differences were discussed in this chapter.

The three principal ways by which a nongraded program can be implemented were also discussed. They were: (1) by providing multi-level instruction in self-contained, heterogeneous classes; (2) by assigning children to self-contained classes according to performance levels and then providing instruction from one class to the next on different levels of difficulty; and (3) by regrouping a large aggregation of children from time to time during the day or week to form clusters or classes that work on different levels under the direction of different teachers. Plan 3 could be either a departmentalized program or one involving team teaching.

It was suggested that administrative leadership is essential if the nongraded approach is to be introduced in a school. A change from a graded to a nongraded program would require that additional instructional materials be purchased and that changes be made in various school-wide policies. In the typical school, it is not possible for teachers themselves to take action in these areas. The teachers must wait for decisions made by the administrative personnel. Thus, if changes are to be implemented, the administrative staff will have to take the initiative.

# 2

# The Nongraded Movement in Perspective

## Introduction

Although the term _nongraded school_ has only recently come into common usage, most of the practices which have been suggested as ways to implement this plan are not new. Some of them have been advocated for more than one hundred years. In this chapter, the more important of these practices are described and an attempt is made to relate them to the nongraded approach.

## Breaking the Lockstep of the Graded School

For the past one hundred years the graded school has been the dominant pattern of elementary school organization in America. Weaknesses in this plan for curriculum and instruction have been the principal reason for interest in the nongraded approach. The graded elementary school came into popular use in America during the middle of the 1800's. It represented a new way to organize the educational program. Prior to that time, the predominant plan was the one-room school in which instruction was nongraded.[1]

---

[1]Edwin Grant Dexter, A History of Education in the United States (New York: The Macmillan Company, 1919), Chap. xi. See also Walter H. Small, Early New England Schools (Boston: Ginn and Company, Publishers, 1914), Chaps. iii and ix.

In this early type of school, there were children of various ages in the one classroom, and achievement levels varied a great deal. Instruction was differentiated, that is, the teacher gave different assignments to different children. While one child or several pupils did certain work in a subject, others who were ready for more advanced study were assigned such work by the teacher. Thus a number of different levels were being studied simultaneously by pupils in the same classroom. Classes were often smaller than the typical class of thirty today.

During the first half of the 1800's, certain persons in the growing urban centers of the East felt that the one-room school was inadequate to meet the rising tide of enrollments. Building many one-room schools, similar to those already in existence, would be expensive. It was necessary to find a way to educate large numbers of children at less cost. In some cities, a plan was tried whereby a hundred or more children were placed in one large classroom, and older pupils were used as teacher assistants to help with instruction. With so many children in one large classroom, a natural outcome was the separation of the pupils into older and younger groups. Thus, the practice of age-level groupings began to occur.[2] Although this was a new practice in America, it had been tried for some time in certain European schools.

The next logical step was to build two separate rooms — one for the older children and one for the younger ones. This is exactly what was done in some of the city schools. At first, just two age divisions were tried; then three, four, and more were introduced. The Quincy Grammar School, built in Boston in 1848, is said to be the first that was designed from the start to provide separate classrooms for children at each age level. There was a separate teacher for each age group. Since it was felt that all of the pupils in a given room could be taught the same thing, class size in many of the graded schools was allowed to become large. This meant that the per-pupil-cost of education could be kept very low. It was necessary to keep it low because it was difficult to secure money for public schools. Another factor which contributed to the development of the graded school in the United States was the publication, during the first half of the nineteenth century, of the first graded textbook series.

---

[2]Dexter, *A History of Education in the United States*, Chap. xi. Also see Ellwood P. Cubberly, *Public Education in the United States* (Boston: Houghton Mifflin Company, 1947), Chap. v.

Ever since the graded program became firmly established, an ever-increasing number of educators have pointed out its weaknesses and suggested plans to overcome them.[3] The chief weakness in the theory of the graded school is its disregard for children's individual differences. Just because children are the same chronological age and thus assigned to the same grade, does not mean that they are all capable or ready to do the same work during the year. Yet this is exactly what is expected in the graded plan. The critics claim that this program perpetuates an injustice on the above average students, for they are held back, while below average students are faced with work that is too hard and they experience failure. The slower pupils are then submitted to further discouragement by being retained and forced to repeat the work of the grade. The critics have dubbed the graded program the *lockstep plan* — the whole class moves ahead together, with everyone expected to do the same thing in the same period of time.

Many plans have been suggested to break the lockstep pattern of the graded school and to provide more adequately for individual differences. Certain elements of nongrading have been embodied in most of these. As early as the 1860's, William T. Harris, Superintendent of Schools in St. Louis and later Commissioner of Education for the United States, introduced a plan of more frequent promotions and retentions as a way to provide more adequately for children of different ability.[4] The decision to promote or retain children was made several times a year, instead of just once each year. Students of exceptional ability did not have to wait so long to be double-promoted, and when they were, they skipped only part of a year's work instead of a full year. Pupils who were progressing very slowly did not have to struggle through an entire year of failure before being retained and placed with children who were working at more nearly their level. The plan resulted in certain aspects of the lockstep being broken, but the nongraded idea was only partially involved because the children in a given class or section were usually held together for all of their work.

*Multi-track* programs of one kind or another have been devised as another way to break the lockstep pattern of school organization. One example was the Cambridge Plan of the early 1900's in which the majority of children pursued the elementary program in a

---

[3]William S. Gray, "The Evolution of Patterns of Instructional Organization," in *Reading Instruction in Various Patterns of Grouping,* ed. Helen M. Robinson (Chicago: The University of Chicago Press, 1959), pp. 14-19.

[4]William W. Holmes, *School Organization and the Individual Child* (Worcester, Massachusetts: The Davis Press, 1912), Chap. iii.

standard number of years while the more able students constituted a separate group which was helped to progress through the program in less than the standard length of time.[5] An important feature of this organizational scheme was that it provided for the different rates at which children could learn. Another variation was the Santa Barbara Plan of about the same time in history.[6] Here, the pupils were divided into three tracks, but all of the boys and girls remained in the elementary program for the same number of years. Children in the three tracks studied the same basic topics at the same time, but the pupils in the second and third tracks studied the topics in greater depth. An important feature of this organizational scheme was that it provided for variations in the content which children of different ability were expected to learn. The well-known Detroit XYZ Plan of the 1920's contained this feature, and in addition, the more able pupils were helped to progress through the topics at a faster rate than the slower children.[7]

Each of these multi-track programs was an attempt to break the lockstep, but the nongraded approach was only partially implemented because sufficient attention was not given to helping individual children in a given track progress at their own rates. All of the pupils in a given track were expected to do the same thing in the same length of time. And there was usually no provision for the child who performed at one level in reading and a different level in arithmetic. A child in a given track was expected to do all of his work in the different subjects on the same level of difficulty.

Today, variations of these plans are employed in many schools.[8] Sometimes instead of referring to them as multi-track programs, the terms *inter-classroom achievement grouping* or *ability grouping* are used.

In the 1880's Preston Search devised a program of individual progress as a way to break the lockstep. He introduced his plan in the schools of Pueblo, Colorado.[9] An attempt was made to help individual children in a class do the work for which they were

---

[5]Ibid.

[6]Ibid.

[7]Stuart A. Courtis, "Ability Grouping in Detroit Schools," in *Adapting the Schools to Individual Differences,* Twenty-fourth Yearbook of the National Society for the Study of Education, Part II (Bloomington, Illinois: Public School Publishing Company, 1925), pp. 44-47.

[8]For one example see Carl F. Hansen, *The Amidon Elementary School* (Englewood Cliffs, New Jersey: Prentice-Hall, Inc., 1962), Chap. i.

[9]Henry J. Otto, "Instructional Organization of Schools," in *Encyclopedia of Educational Research,* ed. Walter S. Monroe (New York: The Macmillan Company, 1941), p. 434.

ready. The plan clearly embodied the essence of the nongraded approach.

Since 1900 an increasing number of educators have attempted to break away from the lockstep program of the graded school. The battle has been an uphill one, however, for the graded plan has persisted and is still firmly entrenched in many places. It also has the advantage of being a very simple plan to administer, and it is by far the easiest type of program for a teacher to conduct. Because of these circumstances, many teachers and administrators cling to the graded plan even though it appears not to be the best type of instructional program for children.

Early in the 1900's Frederic Burk followed Search's lead and developed a program of individual progress at the San Francisco Normal School.[10] This was a major effort by Burk and his staff to break the lockstep. The children studied individualized, self-instructional materials prepared by the staff. Later, Carleton Washburne, one of Burk's associates, transplanted the idea to the Winnetka Public Schools. There, beginning in 1919, Washburne led the staff in the development of one of the most thoroughly nongraded programs that has yet to be devised.[11] The nongraded approach, which consisted of helping each child progress at the level where he was, permeated the entire school program. Not only was it practiced in the skill subjects with the now famous Winnetka materials for self-instruction,[12] but in the group and creative activities as well, which included social studies, science, art, shop, music, and physical education. It was also evident in various all-school enterprises conducted by the boys and girls, and especially in the extensive guidance and mental health program that was developed.

The Winnetka materials for self-instruction were akin to what we now refer to as *programed instruction.* The topics to be learned were arranged sequentially in small steps or lessons. Simple directions for each step were written especially for children. Each new

---

[10]Mary A. Ward, et al., "Individual System As Developed in the San Francisco State Teachers College," in *Adapting the Schools to Individual Differences,* Twenty-fourth Yearbook of the National Society for the Study of Education, Part II (Bloomington, Illinois: Public School Publishing Company, 1925), pp. 60-77.

[11]John L. Tewksbury, "An Historical Study of the Winnetka Public Schools from 1919 to 1946" (unpublished Doctoral dissertation, Northwestern University, 1962).

[12]Gertrude Hildreth, "Individual Differences," in *Encyclopedia of Educational Research,* ed. Walter S. Monroe (New York: The Macmillan Company, 1941), p. 599.

process was carefully explained in simple language. Practice exercises were provided, and the child was expected to check his work himself.

The contributions of Washburne, Burk, and Search are often not given an adequate place in the history of nongrading because these men, in their speaking and writing, made little use of the term *nongraded*. They referred instead to the lockstep pattern of the graded school and to their particular plans for individualizing instruction as a means to break this pattern. But a study of these plans reveals clearly that they were attempts to develop programs that were thoroughly nongraded.

In recent years, an increasing number of self-instructional materials have become available commercially. Not only do they involve auto-instruction but also self-checking. The term *programed instruction* is often used to refer to them. They are sold in such forms as workbooks, teaching machines, and large multi-level pamphlet sets. In each case, the child studies at his own rate. Such materials are useful, and in fact necessary, in a nongraded program where children work at different levels on a given subject. The teacher cannot himself provide all of the instruction on these different levels — he must supplement his own efforts with materials that are self-directive and that the pupils can study and check on their own. The fact that more of these teaching materials are now becoming available commercially contributes to interest in nongrading, because they are of great help to a teacher in conducting this type of program.

It was not until the 1940's that the term *nongraded,* or *ungraded,* came into usage in connection with certain programs designed to break the lockstep of the graded school.[13] One of the first places where the term was used was in the schools of Milwaukee. The program there was inaugurated in the early 1940's and continues in existence today.[14] In the intervening years it has received considerable publicity. The public school system of Park Forest, Illinois, is another of those frequently credited with being one of the early systems to develop a plan of curriculum and instruction specifically identified as *nongraded.*[15] This occurred in the late 1940's. Since then, many educators have expressed interest in the program.

---

[13] John I. Goodlad and Robert H. Anderson, *The Nongraded Elementary School,* rev. ed. (New York: Harcourt, Brace & World Inc., 1963), p. 53.
[14] Florence C. Kelly, "The Primary School in Milwaukee," *Childhood Education,* XXIV (January, 1948), 236-38.
[15] Kent C. Austin, "The Ungraded Primary School," *Childhood Education,* XXXIII (February, 1957), 260-63.

Commencing in the late 1940's, an attempt has been made in an increasing number of schools to modify instructional programs so as to embrace more of the nongraded approach, and the term *nongraded* has been used to describe these programs. As this has occurred, a snowball effect has been created, for as certain aspects of nongrading are introduced in one school, the staffs in neighboring schools hear of the innovation and become curious. Thus, interest spreads from one school to another. A recent example of this is the Detroit Public Schools, where nongraded primary units had been developed in several of the elementary buildings. Then in 1964 a decision was made to expand the program to all of the city's elementary schools.

## Weaknesses of the Graded School

The weaknesses of the graded plan have become more and more obvious with the passing of the years. Today there is considerable evidence which attests to these weaknesses. One of the most important kinds of evidence are the results of standardized tests which clearly show the wide range of pupil performance among the children of a given age in one grade. In one typical first grade, for instance, general reading performance varied in the spring from 1.0 to 2.4. In a fourth grade, the range extended from 2.0 to 6.2. The range in other subjects was almost as great. Variations in intelligence quotients typically range as much as forty to fifty points. For example, I.Q. scores frequently vary from a low of 80 to a high of 120 or 130. Other measures, including those of motor ability and creativity, reveal similar wide ranges in performance levels among children who are the same chronological age and in the same grade. Not only do these differences exist between children, but in the case of a single child the level of his performance in one area may vary considerably from that in a different area.

Educational psychologists, specialists in child development, and certain teachers and administrators have accumulated a mass of evidence which indicates clearly that each child is different.[16]

---

[16]Gertrude Hildreth, "Individual Differences," in *Encyclopedia of Educational Research*, ed. Walter S. Monroe (New York: The Macmillan Company, 1941), pp. 596-602. Although this is an older edition of the *Encyclopedia*, Hildreth's article remains an informative one. See also Albert J. Harris, "Influences of Individual Differences on the Reading Program," in *Meeting Individual Differences in Reading*, ed. H. Alan Robinson (Chicago: The University of Chicago Press, 1964), pp. 17-24.

Given this fact, it is absurd to expect all children in a given grade to do the same work and to complete it during the year they spend in the grade. Yet this is exactly what is suggested by the theory of the graded school.

Teachers and administrators who are not convinced of the extent of variation in the performance levels of children in a given grade, are urged to begin their consideration of nongrading by conducting a study in their own school of children's performance levels. The results of standardized tests can easily be used as the source of the necessary information. In any typical school, the picture that is revealed will be unmistakably clear.

It has always been apparent, of course, to teachers and parents that there is some variation in the way children in a graded class-room perform; but it has been a common belief that these differences in performance could be overcome if the slower pupils would just work harder and if the instruction was better. This line of reasoning is often heard when advocates of the graded school discuss ways to deal with children's individual differences. Research studies, however, do not support this way of thinking. The studies show that when a large group of children of mixed performance levels study harder and have better instruction, the range of differences increases rather than decreases.

In a graded program the children who fail in their effort to do the work of a grade are expected to repeat the work the following year. In the theory of the graded plan this is supposed to be an adequate way to take care of these children. There is now considerable evidence which suggests that this procedure is not particularly effective. In numerous studies of retained children, the large majority of the pupils experienced less growth in subject-matter achievement than comparable students who were promoted.[17] In these studies a number of the retained children actually scored lower on the tests at the end of their repeat year than they had the previous year, whereas this occurred less often with comparable pupils who had been promoted. A small minority of the retained children did do somewhat better than their counterparts who were promoted.

One study suggests that children who are retained make poorer social adjustments and develop poorer self-concepts than children

---

[17]For a brief summary of these studies, including extensive bibliographic references, see Goodlad and Anderson, *The Nongraded Elementary School*, 1963, pp. 34-35, 231-34. Also see Virgil E. Herrick, "Promoting and Reporting Practices," in *Encyclopedia of Educational Research*, ed. Chester W. Harris (The Macmillan Company, 1960), pp. 438-39.

of similar background and ability who are promoted.[18] This study was concerned with the changes that occurred during only one year. Had it continued over a longer period, the results might be even more disturbing. There is reason to believe that failure to do grade-level work, and subsequent nonpromotion, are factors which may contribute to children's desire to want to leave school when they are older and to be "drop outs."

Few persons, adult or child, want to continue doing that at which they are not able to achieve reasonable success. The natural impulse is to want to get out from under this degrading experience, to leave it and find something else at which they can be more successful. Adults usually have the freedom to change from one type of work to another until they find something more in line with their level of readiness and ability. Children in a graded school, however, are not so fortunate. There is only one path that is open, and they are required to follow it. They must continue to work on material which is too hard, to fail, and be nonpromoted. No other alternative exists in the theory of the graded elementary school; a child cannot even quit, for he must be older before he is given this choice. The program seems to be most unreasonable and to discount completely the fact that children differ in many ways in their performance. There appears, then, to be considerable reason to view as one of the weaknesses of the graded school the method that is used to deal with children who progress more slowly than the average.

In the case of especially bright children in a graded program, they can be double-promoted. When this occurs they skip the work of the next higher grade. Having a child skip over the work of an entire year has always been a problem in graded schools, because there is no specific provision for him to receive instruction in the material which he skipped. How much more logical it would be if an especially bright child could work ahead, step by step, into more challenging material without having to skip any of the important steps. But since this approach is not part of the theory of the graded program, we have another weakness in the plan.

The inability of the graded school to provide adequately for individual differences in performance has caused an increasing number of educators to consider modifications in the plan. Some

---

[18]John I. Goodlad, "Some Effects of Promotion and Nonpromotion upon the Social and Personal Adjustment of Children," *Journal of Experimental Education*, XXII (June, 1954), pp. 301-28. Also see pages 37-39 of Goodlad and Anderson's *The Nongraded Elementary School*, 1963.

of the more significant of these were mentioned earlier in the chapter. Included were individualized instruction, schemes to group children according to performance levels, and nongrading. Advocates of nongrading believe that it holds more promise than graded programs for creating an atmosphere in which children may develop more positive attitudes toward themselves, toward learning, toward teachers and other authority figures, and toward the school and other institutions for learning. It would seem as though a child would have a more favorable attitude in these areas if he has reasonable success with his daily work than if he encounters repeated failure with it. In the case of able children in a nongraded program, they may be stimulated by the more challenging work that is presented to them. In a graded school, such pupils may become less interested in their work because it moves so slowly and does not deal with topics in sufficient depth.

## Progressive Education

Two movements in recent years have helped to create a climate of thought which is favorable to the nongraded approach. They are Progressive Education[19] and the mental health movement in education.[20] Both movements represented efforts to overcome weaknesses in traditional school practice; because of this, some of the beliefs that were propounded were similar to those already described in the previous sections of this chapter dealing with the weaknesses of graded schools.

Progressive Education was not a single, clearly defined plan, but instead a collection of many ideas. One of these was the concern that schools provide more adequately for children's individual differences. Another, and certainly one of the most important, was the belief that there should be a freer school environment, one which would be more conducive to nurturing children's creativeness and self-reliance. The Progressives reacted against the program of the traditional elementary school of the early 1900's which was very rigid and entirely pre-planned around adult ideas. They also felt that in the traditional school the child was viewed merely as a depository for skills and information. In contrast to this view,

[19]Carleton Washburne, *What Is Progressive Education* (New York: The John Day Company, 1952).

[20]Carleton Washburne, *A Living Philosophy of Education* (New York: The John Day Company, 1940), Chap. iii.

the Progressives believed that boys and girls were dynamic beings who should be helped to use skills and information in ways that were meaningful to them, and helped to develop and use their own imaginative powers to deal with various situations. The Progressives believed that if the program was more flexible it would provide a better learning environment. This desire for greater flexibility is akin to the interest which many educators of today have for nongrading.

## The Mental Health Movement in Education

Another factor to consider in appraising circumstances which have contributed to the current interest in nongrading is the mental health movement in education. This movement began in the second and third decades of the 1900's, and since then has gained increasing recognition, although even today it is an area with which many teachers and administrators are only vaguely familiar. One of the important concerns in this movement is that each child be helped to develop a positive self-image. Mental health workers, psychologists, pediatricians, social workers, and educators believe that many factors influence a child's self-concept. Most important are the attitudes of parents, peers, and school personnel. Children who are subjected to repeated failure experiences in any one of these areas might be expected to have difficulty forming a positive self-image. Mental health workers believe that the practice of criticizing a child who does not do the work of his grade in school, even though he has put forth effort and made progress at his own level, is damaging to the child's feelings about his own worth. This problem is intensified when a child experiences failure for several years in a row and in more than one subject.

Persons interested in the mental health movement believe that one important factor in helping a child develop positive mental health is to make it possible for him to have a reasonable number of success experiences — certainly more successes than failures. Today, an increasing number of persons have an awareness of factors related to mental health. This awareness provides a background which is favorable to the nongraded approach, because the latter offers a way to help more children have success experiences in school. As more teachers and administrators receive direct training in the mental health approach to education, and as they are influenced by the mental health specialists who work in the schools, more school staff members will have a background which will cause them to be favorably disposed toward nongrading.

## Contributions of Goodlad and Anderson

Any discussion of factors contributing to the growth of interest in nongrading would be incomplete without reference to the work of John I. Goodlad and Robert H. Anderson. Both men have conducted studies regarding various aspects of nongrading and have contributed many publications explaining and advocating this approach to curriculum and instruction. Their scholarly book, *The Nongraded Elementary School*,[21] has enjoyed a wide readership. It presents a convincing rationale for this type of program, and it contains a comprehensive bibliography which is valuable to persons who desire to study this topic in depth. Their book differs from this one in that this author has focused on specific operational procedures in nongraded programs and furnished examples that are in addition to those available elsewhere.

## Possible Advantages of a Nongraded Program

Advocates of nongrading believe that there are a number of advantages to this type of program. Some of those most often cited are:

• Each child is helped to work at his own level of readiness. Therefore he is more likely to have success experiences with his work. In a graded classroom students of lower achievement are often forced to advance to new work with the rest of the class even though they have only a vague understanding of the previous skills. After an extended exposure to this practice, many become discouraged and confused. In a nongraded program, a child does not move on to more difficult topics until he has had reasonable success with the preliminary work. Thus there are fewer gaps in his learning and less reason to become confused.

---

[21]John I. Goodlad and Robert H. Anderson, *The Nongraded Elementary School*, rev. ed. (New York: Harcourt, Brace & World, Inc.), 1963.

• Children are not designated as failures simply because they cannot do work at a certain level. They are not expected to perform tasks for which they are not ready.

• Because of the greater opportunity for children to have success experiences with their work, the pupils may develop a more favorable attitude towards learning, and toward educational institutions and teachers.

• Children who are slow starters in first grade but who later make faster progress, are not penalized for their earlier retardation by being made to repeat first grade.

• When a child has an extended absence, he would not have to miss important work in the skill subjects. He could pick up his studies at the point where he left off before his absence.

• There are fewer gaps in instruction for especially bright children; even though they progress more rapidly they do not skip the work of a given grade. Because these children are helped to progress to work commensurate with their ability, they may find school a challenging experience.

• Children who progress slowly are not failed and then forced to repeat a year's work in the basic skills. Failure and repetition experiences of this type are considered detrimental to the development of constructive attitudes in children.

• The program provides for the wide range of differences which exist between children, and also for differences in an individual child's performance from one subject to the next. In addition it provides for the fact that a child's rate of learning varies from one period to the next as he is growing older. At some times he may make rapid progress whereas at other times he may progress more slowly or remain temporarily on a plateau.

• Children may develop more self-reliance. Since instruction is conducted at different levels for different children in the same classroom, the teacher will be unable to work directly with all of the children all of the time. While he works with a few, the rest must proceed on their own with various activities. More responsibility is placed on the learner, and there is reason to believe that this may foster the development of self-reliance.

• Since the children are not all competing against a uniform standard (grade-level expectancies), it is possible that less emphasis will be placed on comparing how well children measure up to such a standard. Instead, more emphasis can be placed on the progress and effort which an individual child shows regardless of his level.

• Since none of the work in the skill subjects is reserved for a particular year or time, teachers should feel less compelled to push slower children through grade-level work regardless of their lack of readiness. For the same reason, teachers would have no reason to fear that the most capable students, by doing advanced work, would encroach on material reserved for the next teacher.

• Any serious attempt at nongrading will necessitate a reappraisal of what should be taught and what methods of instruction should be employed. Hopefully, such a reappraisal would result in an improved educational program.

## Research Efforts

Many teachers and administrators want to know if there is research evidence which indicates the relative merits of nongrading. A number of studies have been conducted, but in the judgment of this author the results are inconclusive. The principal focus of these studies has been to determine whether children learn more in a nongraded program than they do in a graded one. A close examination of this research reveals that the investigators have had considerable difficulty designing studies that would yield meaningful results.[22] The reason for this is that nongrading involves an approach to education which to be thoroughly implemented involves many different aspects of school practice. Because of its pervasiveness, a great many variables are operative, and it has proved difficult to control all of these in the research efforts.

An important variable that has not been adequately controlled in comparisons of graded and nongraded plans is the type of teaching employed in the two plans. In some of the studies, the word of a school official has been accepted as sufficient to classify a school program as graded or nongraded. No attempt was made by the researcher to specify the instructional practices that were necessary for a program to qualify as one type or the other, nor was anything done to determine whether certain instructional practices were actually employed in the many classes participating in a given study.

---

[22]For a further discussion of some of the problems involved in the design of meaningful research, and for bibliographic references to important studies that have been conducted, see Goodlad and Anderson *The Nongraded Elementary School*, 1963, pp. 214-18, and John I. Goodlad, "Toward Improved School Organization," *The National Elementary Principal*, XLI (December, 1961), 1961 Yearbook, p. 86.

Another variable that has not been adequately controlled in comparing the two approaches is the method of assigning children to classes. The graded and nongraded schools in a particular study should all employ the same method of assigning pupils to teachers. If this is not done, it would be difficult to tell whether the results that were obtained were due to differences between the graded and nongraded approach, or to differences in the way children were assigned to teachers. For instance, if heterogeneous grouping is practiced in some of the schools and inter-classroom achievement grouping is practiced in others, the results may be due more to the differences in grouping than to the differences between the graded and nongraded aspects of the program.

If the variables mentioned above are not carefully controlled, the results of the research will be meaningless. In most of the studies conducted to date, these variables were not adequately handled. Therefore, this author does not believe that it is possible at this time to judge the value of nongrading on the basis of research evidence. We will have to wait for further studies which may be conducted in such a way that the results will be more meaningful. Although we will have to be content with this state of indefiniteness for awhile, we should not forget that there *is* rather definite evidence that a graded program is not a satisfactory way to work with children. This evidence was presented earlier in this chapter. Something else must surely be better, and nongrading may possibly be part of that "something."

One study by Hillson and his associates bears mentioning because it represents an effort at more careful control of some of the variables. In this project, the reading performance of children in graded and nongraded programs was compared.[23] An important feature of this study is that specific attention was given to defining criteria of gradedness and nongradedness, and then selecting classes which met these standards. Preliminary results indicate that children in the nongraded program performed somewhat better.

Most of the studies to date have attempted to evaluate children's performance in the skill subjects, especially reading. There have been few attempts to investigate such important factors as chil-

---

[23]Maurie Hillson and others, "A Controlled Experiment Evaluating the Effects of a Nongraded Organization on Pupil Achievement," in *Change and Innovation in Elementary School Organization: Selected Readings*, ed., Maurie Hillson (New York: Holt, Rinehart, and Winston, 1965), pp. 365-72. This book also contains a collection of several other articles which describe research studies of non-graded programs.

dren's self-concepts, attitudes toward learning, and level of self-reliance. These are important to consider in comparing graded and nongraded programs, and perhaps even more important than reading or arithmetic performance. The fact that changes in these other areas occur slowly, over a period of years rather than months, increases considerably the difficulty of obtaining objective evidence. It is difficult enough to create matched teaching situations for a few months, but when this is attempted for three to six years, the difficulties become enormous. The lack of research to evaluate these various non-academic factors is another reason why it is premature to judge the value of nongrading on the basis of existing studies.

## Summary

In this chapter, an attempt has been made to provide sufficient background information on nongrading to help the reader gain a perspective on the movement. Essentially, nongrading is a reaction to weaknesses in the graded school — a reaction that has been gathering momentum for one hundred years. Although the term nongraded is new, many of the ideas embodied in this approach are not new at all — they have been suggested individually for many years. One of the principal weaknesses of the graded plan is that it does not provide sufficiently for children's individual differences in growth rates and learning capacities. Today more than ever before, extensive evidence is available to verify that such differences exist and are in fact very great. A nongraded program is one in which an attempt is made to work with children at their own levels. It appears that such a program fits very well with the way children really are.

Several other factors were cited as contributing to the present interest in nongrading. These were the influence of Progressive Education, the mental health movement in education, and the published materials of Professors John I. Goodlad and Robert H. Anderson.

To date, research efforts to determine the relative effectiveness of graded and nongraded programs have not yielded results which are particularly meaningful. We are still at the level of having to consider nongrading in the light of claims and theories which seem plausible rather than as a practice clearly supported by the weight of research evidence.

Advocates of nongrading believe that this approach to curriculum organization and instruction holds more promise than does a graded program for creating an atmosphere in which boys and girls may develop more positive attitudes toward themselves, as well as toward teachers, educational institutions, and learning. Positive attitudes in these areas are essential if a growing child is to be able to live successfully in our modern society where continued learning and continued attendance in educational institutions is so essential.

Looking toward the future it seems probable that we will see a continued movement in schools away from the theory of graded programming toward a more nongraded approach. A graded program is just not in harmony with what we know about children, whereas nongrading seems to fit so well with the way children really are. As teachers and administrators introduce instructional and grouping procedures to provide for the wide range of children's individual differences (which is clearly happening on an ever-increasing scale), this very process will represent a move toward nongrading, whether or not one chooses to use this term.

In an earlier chapter, an explanation of the meaning of nongrading was presented. In the chapters which follow the present one, specific procedures in the operation of nongraded programs are discussed. An attempt is made to deal with factors that teachers and administrators would want to think about as they consider whether or not to incorporate more of the nongraded approach in their educational program.

# 3

# *Teaching Procedures in a Nongraded Program*

## Introduction

If an educational program is to be thoroughly nongraded, a different type of instruction is required than the teaching patterns one would expect to find in a graded school. According to the theory of a _graded_ program, the teacher's goal is to have everyone in the class learn only the material reserved for the grade. It is assumed that all of the children are up to a certain level when they enter a grade, and that they should be up to the next grade level by the end of the year. Proceeding on this assumption it is quite natural for a teacher in a graded class to want to teach the pupils as one large group and to move them together during the year through the designated content for the grade. This practice, called _whole-class instruction_, seems to fit well with a graded program. It is the easiest type of program for a teacher to conduct. Since all children in a classroom have the same work to accomplish, there is little reason for the teacher to offer instruction on more than one level — that is, to have more advanced work for some pupils and less complicated material for the others. He would provide instruction on one level for the whole class and all the children would be expected to do it. Whole-class, single-level instruction is the characteristic teaching pattern in a rigidly graded program. This method is frequently referred to as *lockstep* teaching; everyone moves ahead together attempting to do the same assignments in the same length of time.

To conduct a program that is thoroughly nongraded, it is necessary for the instructional procedures to differ from those which have just been described. Two practices would be essential: (1) a teacher must provide multi-level instruction for the children assigned to him, and (2) he must conduct whole-class discussions and projects so that children who perform differently are helped to participate, each in his own way. For the program to be thoroughly nongraded,* the teacher would need to employ these procedures whether he was in a self-contained heterogeneous class, a self-contained class in a homogeneous grouping plan, or in a departmentalized or team teaching arrangement where different clusters or classes of children were assigned to him at different times.

## Multi-Level Instruction: A Method for a Teacher to Use in Working with the Children who are Assigned to Him

The following discussion of multi-level instruction is directed primarily toward work in the skill subjects. There are two principal ways for a teacher to provide instruction of this type for the pupils assigned to him:

(1) He can divide the children into sub-groups with each group working on different materials. The reading groups found in many classes are an example of this method.

(2) He can have the children engage in various forms of individualized instruction. One example of this method is *individualized reading*. Another would be the use of self-directed teaching materials. These have the following characteristics: the topics to be

---

*The reader should recall that in this book a distinction is made between *thoroughly* and *partially* nongraded programs. The term *partially nongraded* refers to programs similar to Plans 2 and 3 (see Chapter One) in which the teacher instructs the children assigned to him in a whole-class, lockstep manner. Whereas the term *thoroughly nongraded* refers to a program in which the teacher provides multi-level instruction for the children who are assigned to him. The latter could occur in either Plan 1, 2, or 3.

learned are arranged sequentially in small steps or lessons; simple directions prepared especially for children are provided for each step; each new process is carefully explained in simple language; practice exercises are provided — usually the child is expected to check his own work with answers that are provided. Examples of these materials would be: (a) locally prepared guides to help students study standard textbooks or workbooks more independently; (b) programed workbooks such as the McGraw-Hill beginning reading materials, the Macmillan reading spectrum, and the Charles E. Merrill reading lab; (c) tape-recorded lessons; (d) filmstrip lessons; (e) the Reader's Digest skill building materials in reading; (f) the Field Enterprises Cyclo-teacher; and (g) the Science Research Associates (SRA) learning laboratories in reading, work-study skills, and maps and globes.

A third type of individualized instruction is *independent study*. Having children use self-instructional materials is one form of independent study. However, when educators use this term they are often referring to something a little different. They are thinking of less structured activities which children, individually or in small groups, develop on their own or by means of teacher-pupil planning. These activities might include engaging in creative writing, developing ways to share a story a child had read, preparing a demonstration, or studying a topic of special interest in one of the skill subjects or content areas of the curriculum. The activity is one that emerges in its own form from some interest or concern a child has. He is encouraged to figure out his own ways to proceed with it, although the teacher will provide guidance if needed. As might be expected, some children are more successful with projects of this type than other pupils.

There is good reason to believe that teachers should do all they can to encourage children in independent study. This type of activity is another way to adapt the educational program to the needs and interests of different pupils. It also encourages children to think on their own and make use of their imaginative powers.

In conducting a program of multi-level teaching in the skill subjects, it would be desirable to use both sub-group instruction and the various forms of individualized instruction which have been described. No one teaching method should be employed exclusively — a variety of methods is more appropriate.

There should be no delusions about the difficulty a teacher will have in providing instruction on a multi-level basis for the children assigned to him. There is no escaping the fact that it represents a more difficult type of teaching than the whole-class, single-level method. A teacher must plan the work of different sub-groups, meet with each of them, and coordinate the use of a wide variety of individualized instruction materials which span several grades. In the subject of reading, for instance, the teacher might meet with each of the sub-groups one to three times a week, but not every day. To provide for the range of children's performance levels, texts from several grades in the basal series could be used. The pupils who at a given time were not meeting in a sub-group with the teacher, could engage in various types of independent work such as: (a) assignments which followed sub-group lessons; (b) individualized reading of supplementary readers or trade books; (c) self-instruction on reading skills by means of locally prepared or commercial materials; (d) self-instruction in other curriculum areas; (e) individual use of tape-recorded lessons and filmstrips in the classroom or in the school's learning materials center; (f) continuing work on an individual or small group project: (g) or other miscellaneous independent work activities.* In these activities, the more capable pupils would be expected to do more than those who learn more slowly.

Teachers might wish to encourage the use of *pupil-team instruction* for some of the seatwork activities. Two or three children could work together, helping and checking each other as they proceed with self-directed study materials. Pupil-team arrangements are regarded by some teachers as an effective way to organize certain children for independent work activities.

In arithmetic, the core of the program could be individualized, either by the use of self-instructive commercial materials, or locally prepared guides to accompany the texts or workbooks in a basal series. Children might do some of their work in pupil-team arrangements. The teacher could meet with sub-groups on certain days to provide variety, motivation, and additional instruction on difficult concepts. Each group would not meet every day, however, for the self-instructional materials would carry some of the teaching load.

The reading and arithmetic examples just presented are not intended to suggest that multi-level instruction must be conducted

---

*For further discussion of independent work activities which are pupil initiated and which encourage the use of a child's own ideas to create and interpret, see Jeannette Veatch, *Reading in the Elementary School* (New York: The Ronald Press Company, 1966), Chap. v. Also see Helen Fisher Darrow and R. Van Allen, *Independent Activities for Creative Learning* (New York: Bureau of Publications, Teachers College, Columbia University, 1961). Fifty-one activities are described.

in the exact manner described. The examples could be changed by giving a different emphasis to certain of the activities. For instance, less use might be made of basal readers and greater emphasis placed on the language experience approach and individualized reading.

For a nongraded program to be thoroughly implemented, it is essential that the school system provide the materials the teacher will need to conduct multi-level instruction. The materials in the typical graded classroom will not be sufficient. Texts at both higher and lower levels will have to be made available, as well as additional library books. Self-instructional workbooks, tape-recorded lessons, and learning laboratories that extend over several grade levels will have to be provided in large quantities since graded schools have few, if any, of these teaching aids. Although there is not presently a sufficient variety of commercial materials available for multi-level instruction, more are being developed. As these come on the market, another obstacle to the greater individualization of instruction will have been overcome. A school's administrative leaders and board members must be prepared to finance the purchase of the necessary materials. The expense involved might well be an item of major proportion during the several years of the transition from a graded program to a nongraded one.

It is entirely unreasonable to expect teachers to assume the added burden of multi-level instruction without the necessary materials to do so. They should not be expected to secure or develop the materials themselves, for this is too much to ask. Possibly, however, certain interested staff members could be employed in the summer to prepare local guides to make basal texts and workbooks self-instructive, or to evaluate and select commercial materials for self-instruction. It might be desirable to conduct short workshops to help teachers become familiar with the new materials and their use. There would probably be a need for training activities of some sort, because many teachers will be concerned about having to change their instructional procedures and will need assistance and encouragement to do so. If workshops were held prior to the opening of school, teachers might receive extra remuneration for participating. Unless money is available in a school system to finance these activities and to purchase multi-level teaching materials, it will be difficult, if not impossible, for the teachers to implement a thoroughly nongraded program. Teachers will look to their administrative staff to provide the leadership that will be needed to secure sufficient funds to support a nongraded program.

Class size is another factor to think about if a school is seriously considering a move toward a program that is thoroughly nongraded. Room enrollment can be larger in a graded school where there is whole-class, single-level instruction, because the teacher is not as concerned about providing for individual differences. When a teacher must conduct instruction on various levels in order to work with sub-groups of children or individual children at the levels where they are, a class that is too large seriously impedes this effort. Small classes will definitely facilitate the implementation of the nongraded approach. Obviously, the teacher can do little about such a matter since reduction in class size, if it is to occur, will require administrative leadership.

Other ways to help teachers do a more effective job of individualizing instruction have been developed in some schools. In one, for instance, the daily program is conducted so that half of the pupils begin at 8:45 and the rest do not arrive until 9:45. In the afternoon the early group leaves one hour sooner than the others. Thus for two hours a day a teacher has a smaller class with which to work and can be less concerned about providing seatwork for those children with whom he is not working directly.

In another school, teaching assistants are employed. An assistant helps children who are working on self-instructional materials or small group projects. He also keeps track of some of the varied learning materials and corrects some of the paper work. This gives the teacher more opportunity to work with other children. A teaching assistant might not spend all day in one room, but could divide his time between several rooms.

Introduction of instructional procedures appropriate for a nongraded program will bring pressure for change in other aspects of a school's operation. Teachers and administrators will very likely find it necessary to review certain decisions about curriculum content. Over a period of time this could require considerable thought.

Revisions in the reporting system would also be necessary. If instruction is conducted in such a way that individual differences are accepted and provided for, it would hardly be fitting to have a reporting system in which the major emphasis was on rating children against a grade level standard. One important aspect of a new reporting system would be to show the progress each child was making at his own level. Considerable emphasis should be given to this, although other information might also be presented. A sample report form is described in Chapter Six.

Since changes in reporting practices involve total school policy it is likely that leadership from members of the administrative staff will be necessary before changes can be effected. Teachers may recommend certain revision; but without administrative support and leadership, teachers are often not very successful in bringing about changes that go beyond their immediate classrooms.

From the preceding discussion of multi-level instruction, it should be apparent that many factors must be considered and many changes introduced before a thoroughly nongraded program can be established. The changes that are necessary are not easy ones to implement. Even with adequate administrative leadership and financial support, the development of a thoroughly nongraded program will not be an easy task. The reason for this is that no matter how much help a teacher has, a multi-level instructional program will be more difficult to conduct than one which consists primarily of single-level, whole-class instruction. Without a doubt, the greatest obstacle standing in the way of the more rapid adoption of nongrading is that it is hard to conduct this type of program.

## Varying the Content in Multi-Level Instruction

When teachers and administrators consider developing a program of multi-level instruction in the skill subjects, it frequently happens that attention is directed first toward providing for children's individual differences in _rate_ of learning. Very often the program that is developed is one in which the material to be studied is the same for all children — only the rate at which they proceed through the material varies. Most of the commercial materials which are designed for self-instruction, such as programmed workbooks, are also organized this way. Some pupils can proceed rapidly up through the levels or steps, while others go at a slower pace. A faster child, or sub-group of children, might proceed into levels which in a graded school had been reserved for the next higher grade. This child would begin his work the following school year at whatever point he had reached the previous June. The fact that boys and girls are allowed to progress at varying rates would appear to be a distinct improvement over a rigidly graded program where all children are held together.

Desirable as it may be to provide variation in rate, this deals with only one dimension of the individual differences of children. It should also be possible to vary the _content_ for children of different learning patterns. Although there would probably be a basic program through which most children would proceed (at varying rates), the work for the capable children might offer richer opportunities to explore ideas and to dig more deeply into them. Instruction for the less capable pupils would offer a simpler treatment of ideas. As an example, the exercises and discovery situations that would be provided for an able learner in multiplication could require deeper understanding and more insight than the work a less able student would be expected to do when he was ready for the lessons on multiplication. This type of variation could be provided by the teacher in sub-group instruction, as some have regularly done in their work with different reading groups. The same type of differentiated work could be provided by self-instruction materials, but presently there are few materials of this type available commercially. Individualized reading, involving the self-selection of supplementary readers and trade books, results in this same type of differentiated approach. The less able children tend to read less complicated books, while the more able pupils tend toward books that to be appreciated require deeper understanding and insight. Independent study activities provide another way for different children to have diversified learning experiences.

It should be clear, then, that multi-level instruction can provide for differences in the rate at which children progress, and it can also provide qualitative variations in the content. Thus when one pictures a series of levels, one after the other, through which boys and girls are helped to progress, the content of each step would not necessarily have to be identical for everyone.

Although multi-level instruction would comprise an important part of the daily program in a nongraded classroom, the entire school day would not be taken up with learning activities of this type. Other parts of the day would be devoted to whole-class activities.

## Whole-Class Activities

The second instructional procedure that is essential for a program to be thoroughly nongraded is to have whole-class activities conducted in such a way that each child is helped to participate in ways suitable for him. Several examples may serve to illustrate how this can be done. At sharing or newstime, each child can be urged to make a contribution. As he does so, he is likely to select something that is at his own level of understanding. In class discussions pertaining to unit activities, such as teacher-pupil planning sessions or the discussion of a film, the teacher can call on some of the less able children first to give them an opportunity to contribute ideas. On other occasions these boys and girls can be invited to react to the ideas submitted by some of the more capable children. When children of different backgrounds and abilities participate in a class discussion, there will naturally be a range in the complexity of the ideas presented, but each child will contribute on a level that has meaning to him — and each will take from the discussion those things which he is able to understand. Slower pupils may not fully grasp all the insights contributed by the more able students. Although this might be a cause for concern to the teacher in a graded program, the teacher in a nongraded school would accept it as a normal result of children's differences. He would not expect that all children should perform according to a certain standard. Instead, variations are expected, and the teacher would do his best to help children of different levels of performance respect one another and feel comfortable together.

Work in social studies and science can be conducted so that boys and girls of varying abilities study a given topic together. In social studies, for instance, a whole class might study the topic of transportation. Instructional materials of varying difficulty could be used for individual work and sub-group instruction. The more capable children would be helped to pursue the study of transportation in greater depth, while pupils who were at an earlier stage of readiness would be helped to engage in information-gaining and expressional activities that were less complicated. In whole-class discussions, each member could be urged to contribute something that he had learned working on his own level. As various ideas were contributed, and then clarified and expanded by the teacher, each child would perceive these in terms of his own degree of readiness. Other whole-class activities in social studies and science might include viewing visual aids, meeting with a resource person, listening to material read by the teacher, and going on a fieldtrip. In each of these activities, the individual pupil could function at his own level by contributing and taking from the experience that which was meaningful to him.

If all of the work in school was conducted by whole-class activities in the manner described above, the slower children might easily become discouraged. However, if whole-class work is combined with multi-level instruction at other times during the school day, this variety of learning activities would provide slower children with opportunities to be successful on their own level in certain activities, and also to have social interaction in other activities with boys and girls of all abilities.

To help students become more proficient in the various work-study skills useful in studying the social sciences and science, self-teaching, multi-level materials could be provided. Pupils might work on these in addition to engaging in other activities teachers might wish to conduct to help the children improve their work-study skills.

## A Weakness of Self-Instruction Materials

In the foregoing discussion of teaching procedures in nongraded schools, reference has been made to the use of various individualized, self-instructive, learning materials. It was indicated that if a teacher was to conduct a program of multi-level instruction for the pupils assigned to him it would be necessary to make considerable use of such materials. Unfortunately, these materials are not without their weaknesses. One weakness stems from the fact that the work for the children has been pre-planned by an adult, with the result that the children have only to absorb it and respond to certain pre-determined exercises bit by bit. Of course, this weakness is not confined to self-teaching materials, for it is also a problem associated with most standard textbooks and workbooks that are used in elementary schools. Learning of this type does not require that boys and girls be involved in planning goals and using their own ideas and initiative to pursue these goals. There is little opportunity to improve skills of social interaction, and the exercises themselves usually do not involve pupils in the application of learnings in meaningful activities growing out of the children's special interests and concerns.

To provide these desired experiences, self-instruction work should be balanced by activities in sub-groups. Here there is opportunity for social interaction and for the teacher to help pupils make pertinent applications. It is also possible for boys and girls in a sub-group to plan certain aspects of the work on a given topic and then by trial and error to explore the topic in various ways. Through such experiences, the pupils are not only helped to become more self-reliant, but there are opportunities for creative and imaginative thinking. Sub-group activities are not the only way to balance the weakness of self-instructional materials. Other ways include independent study experiences, a program of individualized reading, and various whole-class activities such as those discussed in the previous section of this chapter.

In a balanced program embracing a variety of learning activities, there would definitely be a place for self-instructive materials. They provide children who are working on different levels with a continuing and worthwhile program of individual work. They make it possible for the teacher to work with sub-groups while the rest of the class go about appropriate tasks on their own. It would be unrealistic to expect a teacher to develop seatwork for all of his children that was both self-instructional and on different levels of difficulty. A teacher would hardly have time to do this! Materials that were prepared commercially or locally would surely be necessary. If a teacher did not have to devote so much time to the preparation of seatwork, he would have more time to help children individually or in small groups, and more time to spend on other creative aspects of his teaching. Self-instruction materials provide one of the easiest ways for teachers to break away from the lock-step method of whole-class, single-level instruction. Ways to make a teacher's work easier in a nongraded program merit serious consideration because such a program is inherently more difficult to conduct than a graded one.

## Summary

For an educational program to be thoroughly nongraded, it is necessary that instructional procedures differ from those one would expect to find in a graded school. According to the theory of a graded program, all the children in a classroom are expected to learn the same things during their nine-month stay in the room. Therefore it is not unreasonable for teachers to want to teach all the pupils in the room as one large group and to move them together through the designated content for the grade. This is known as the whole-class, single-level method of instruction. It is a common method of teaching in graded schools. A thorough implementation of nongrading would require that different teaching procedures be used. Two practices would be essential: (1) A teacher must provide multi-level instruction for the children assigned to him, and (2) he must conduct whole-class discussions and projects so that children of different abilities are helped to participate, each in his own way.

There are two principal ways for a teacher to provide multi-level instruction for the children assigned to him: (1) he can divide the children into sub-groups with each group working on different materials, and (2) he can have the children engage in individualized instruction. A teacher would probably want to utilize both procedures. Multi-level teaching is more difficult for teachers than the whole-class, single-level approach. For teachers to utilize this method successfully would require considerable support from members of the administrative staff. It would be necessary for administrative personnel to provide leadership in (1) supplying teachers with the many new teaching materials that would be needed, (2) reducing class size so that a teacher could conduct more sub-group and individualized instruction, and (3) changing the reporting procedures so that the main emphasis would no longer be on rating children against a grade level standard. Even with adequate administrative leadership and financial support, it is not an easy task to conduct a thoroughly nongraded program — multi-level instruction is more difficult for the teacher than single-level, whole-class instruction.

The second instructional procedure that is essential for a program to be thoroughly nongraded is to have whole-class activities conducted in such a way that each child is helped to participate in a manner suitable for him. This is certainly not a new approach, for some teachers have always attempted to employ it. Whether it may be a story the teacher has read to the children, a filmstrip they have viewed, or a discussion of a social studies or science topic, children of different backgrounds and abilities will be able to gain from the activity or contribute to it at their own level of understanding. Some may be able to deal with the ideas in considerable depth whereas others will work with the ideas on a simpler level. So long as the teacher and the school system accept that children will differ in their depth of performance, and all children are not expected to perform up to grade level standard, then the spirit of the nongraded approach would prevail.

# 4

# The Levels Plan of Curriculum Organization in Nongraded Schools

## Introduction

Although most elementary programs today are more graded than nongraded, the latter approach is being tried in an increasing number of schools. To implement a nongraded program, the teachers and administrators in some of these schools have developed what is known as a *levels* plan of curriculum organization in the skill subjects. The levels idea is one that seems to fit naturally with nongrading. In this chapter attention is focused on how the levels plan works. Criticisms of the plan are also discussed.

In this author's survey of published materials dealing with nongrading, there was frequent mention of the use of the levels plan. However, there did not appear to be descriptions or criticisms of the plan which were sufficiently detailed. Because of this, it seemed appropriate to include the present chapter.

In a thoroughly nongraded program, the teacher attempts to help the children assigned to him begin their work at the different levels where they are, and then to make as much progress as they can. By the end of the year, not all of the children will have done the same assignments or completed the same textbooks. However, in a nongraded program this is expected and accepted. Obviously, in this type of a program, a wide range of instruction must be provided. In order that there be a certain element of organization to this instruction and to help teachers keep a closer record of where different children are in the overall curriculum of skills, many schools have divided the curriculum into smaller segments, often referred to as levels. One child may be working at one level while another child studies at a different one. A single pupil may be doing more advanced work in arithmetic but studying at a lower level in reading. There are so many possible variations that teachers and administrators have felt the need for a structure within which to operate. The levels plan provides this structure. This framework is also useful in interpreting children's work to parents at reporting time.

Another reason for organizing the work into smaller segments has been the feeling that the traditional grade designations represent too large a block of work and that smaller segments would be more advantageous. Children would not have to spend so much time at any one level and could experience, more often, the feeling of satisfaction that comes with the successful completion of a section of work.

## The Levels Plan in the Skill Subjects

Reading has usually been the first subject in which the levels plan has been introduced. A typical arrangement is one in which the title of each book in the basal reading series identifies a particular level. There may be as many as fourteen books (levels) which correspond to the work of the three primary years in a typical graded school. A child must be able to read reasonably well at one stage before he can proceed to the next. Children who have considerable ability would be able to advance to work which would have been reserved for the next higher grade in a graded school.

To determine a child's readiness for the next level, tests, teacher judgment, or a combination of both could be used. It would not always be necessary for children to read all of the stories in the reader at a particular level before moving on. If a child could read successfully a sampling of stories in the latter part of his reader, or other stories equivalent to these, this could serve as a demonstration of his ability to perform the skills at this level, and he could then be encouraged to move on to the next.

That reading is generally the first subject to be arranged in levels results from three factors. First, the many books in the basal reading series, more than one per grade, constitute a convenient way to divide the work into segments, each one a little more difficult than the previous. Second, many teachers are accustomed to providing reading instruction on three levels by means of reading groups. Third, supplementary materials are often available so that children can work at their desks in reading materials of different levels of difficulty while the teacher meets with one of the sub-groups. The supplementary materials most frequently available are other readers, trade books from the library, and workbooks or practice sheets of one type or another.

If a teacher is expected to conduct sub-group instruction, it is necessary that learning materials on different levels be available to the children who remain at their desks, especially materials which require a minimum of teacher direction. When children have learning activities which they can pursue without being dependent upon the teacher for directions, the teacher can give more of his attention to the sub-groups. By the time children complete the pre-primers, many are ready to begin using self-instructional and self-checking materials for some of their learning activities.

There are fewer schools where a levels plan has been developed in the other skill subjects of arithmetic, spelling, and handwriting. One reason for this is that teachers are not as accustomed to providing differentiated (multi-level) instruction in these subjects as in reading. Teachers are more in the habit of using the method of whole-class, single-level instruction where all children in the room are expected to do the same work. Another reason is that the basal texts are printed so that there is only one volume per year. Teachers and administrators tend to think of a given textbook as a single body of content rather than to view the content in sections. A third explanation is that in these subjects, materials on different levels which students can use independently for self-instruction have not been readily available to teachers.

If ready-made materials for individualized instruction are not available, it is more difficult to conduct a multi-level instructional program. The reason for this is that without self-teaching materials, there might not be enough for children to do at their desks while the teacher met with different sub-groups. It is not reasonable to expect a teacher to prepare and explain all of the individualized materials himself, and do this on different levels — this would be too time consuming. Nor is it reasonable to expect him to correct all of the practice materials on different levels which the children, working on their own, will turn out. Although the teacher might prepare and correct some of this independent work (especially that which followed up instruction in a sub-group) ready-made, multi-level, self-teaching, self-checking materials would also be necessary. A few publishers are now beginning to have such materials for sale, but the selection is still quite limited. Shortly, however, more of these materials will be available. Before teachers can be expected to use them, however, it will be necessary for a school's administrative staff to take the leadership in securing the materials and suggesting ways to use them in a program of multi-level instruction.

As an aid to those who may be considering a levels plan in arithmetic, spelling, and handwriting as part of a thoroughly nongraded program, the following illustrations are provided. Each example is meant to stimulate thinking rather than to prescribe a single most desirable plan. In all probability, the reader will not agree with all of the procedures in these examples; nevertheless, they may help him to understand better some of the problems involved and stimulate him to think of other procedures which may be desirable.

In arithmetic each level could consist of a section of the basal text or workbook. Each book could be divided into five to eight sections. From a child's standpoint there would appear to be advantages in having the book divided into sections (levels), each of which would take only part of the school year to complete. Many children can work better on goals which are closer than those which are far removed in time. The staff of a school would decide which chapters to include in each level. If names or numbers were used to identify the levels, there would be no need to refer to the grade names printed on each book. Textbook publishers could contribute to the nongraded movement by omitting grade names from books. The usual work of the first three grades might be divided into fifteen to twenty-four levels.

The children assigned to a given teacher could progress from one section to the next at varying rates. Children of considerable ability would be able to advance to levels which would have been reserved for the next higher grade in a graded school. The teacher could meet with sub-groups on certain days. Pupils who were not meeting with the teacher could work individually or in pupil-team arrangements on assignments made in a sub-group or they could study self-instructional materials. The latter would consist of commercial materials and/or locally-prepared guides that would make certain parts of the arithmetic textbook or workbook self-instructional. A group of teachers could be employed in the summer to prepare the guides. Whatever materials are used, there should be provision for the students themselves to check all or most of their practice work.

An examination of arithmetic workbooks will reveal that some of them have been written in a manner that is more nearly self-directive than others. In one series, for instance, the format along with the simplified organization and the carefully planned development of discovery activities, are such that only a limited amount of additional explanation would be needed to enable many of the children to progress on their own. Obviously, to prepare a guide for one of these workbooks would be easier than for one that required too much explanation.

At present there are only a few companies which produce materials specifically designed for self-instruction in arithmetic at the elementary level. Among them are The Webster Division of McGraw-Hill Book Company, Harcourt, Brace & World, Inc., Grolier, Inc., and Scholastic Book Services. The materials sold by these companies do not present a complete arithmetic program, but are intended to be supplementary. Certain pupils could use them for individualized study. When self-instructional materials are produced as a part of basal arithmetic series, this will make it easier for teachers to conduct multi-level instruction.

The program in spelling could also be organized in much the same way. For example: The basic study materials for each level might consist of several lessons from the basal spelling text or workbook. Each level would be identified by a number or a name: first might be *Readiness Activities*, second could be *30 Words*, and the next would be *60 Words*, (the first 30 plus 30 more). Identifying the levels in this way would make it unnecessary to refer to the books by their grade names.

Children would begin the spelling program after they had reached a certain level in reading. Pupils would be allowed to advance at their own rate through the levels, and in some instances they would advance to lessons that would have been reserved for the next higher grade in a graded school. Some might be able to do two lessons a week, while others (of less ability) might spend two weeks on a single lesson. It would take the latter children longer to complete a level, but this would be acceptable in a nongraded program. The different trial tests and final tests that would be needed by individual boys and girls could be administered by some of the reliable and more self-reliant children. Some of the students might be paired for pupil-team instruction in spelling.

Although the use of texts or workbooks as the core of the spelling program may not be an imaginative approach to the teaching of the subject, these materials are nevertheless a dominant part of spelling instruction in the majority of elementary schools. Since this book was written to help teachers and administrators understand ways to introduce nongrading into a typical school program, the workbook approach to spelling was chosen rather to describe a more creative but less representative program.

At present there are few commercial materials specifically designed for self-instruction in spelling, although SRA offers a program beginning at the fourth grade level. Many of the workbooks from regular spelling series, however, can be used reasonably well in a program of individualized study. The pattern of work from lesson to lesson is similar enough in these books so that once introduced to the program many children are able to proceed on their own.

The curriculum in handwriting could also be organized by levels. In the primary years, for example, there might be fifteen levels consisting of sections of handwriting workbooks used in first through third grade. Additional sections, for advanced students, could be included from the fourth grade workbook. The standard of proficiency necessary to complete a given segment of the program could be allowed to vary. A pupil would progress from one level to the next when he could show that his handwriting had improved from what it was when he began that level. Another child whose handwriting was not nearly so well executed might also complete the same section, provided he too was improving.

The standard of proficiency for a given level would be allowed to vary because not all pupils in primary school will be able to write with a high degree of neatness, even after considerable practice. If the standard for a given level was the same for all, it would take some children several years to complete the first few levels. Such slow progress would be discouraging. The goal of the handwriting program in the primary unit is to help each child to learn to write and to improve his handwriting as much as possible with a reasonable amount of practice. Some students will become proficient with minimum practice, whereas others may work long and hard, and although they improve, they may not be able to write very legibly.

If a particular child could write especially well, he would be excused from further practice for several months. At the end of that time he could complete several exercises at the next higher level in the workbook series to determine whether he needed to begin practicing again. Each time an individual was excused from practice for several months, a notation would be made in the teacher's record book that he had moved to the next higher level.

Handwriting workbooks are used in this illustration because they provide a structure for conducting a multi-level instructional program. The structure consists of practice exercises of increasing difficulty, and a definite pattern of work procedures which facilitate progress in a more independent manner than in the case of complete dependence on teacher-prepared lessons and directions. Ready-made study and practice materials which children can use independently, on a continuing basis, are a necessary part of a multi-level instruction program. Used in conjunction with other independent work activities, such materials provide seatwork and free the teacher to meet individually or in small groups with those who are working at different levels.

It would certainly not be necessary for children to do all of the pages in the workbooks. A teacher could modify the program in whatever way seemed desirable. Other types of handwriting practice, including papers written for other subjects, could certainly replace some of the exercises in the workbooks. In fact, some teachers might prefer to conduct the entire handwriting program this way rather than to use workbooks. This could result in an effective program if the children thoroughly understood the type of independent work activities that would promote improved handwriting.

In the preceding discussion of the levels plan, a level has been thought of as consisting of certain instructional materials — specific work which would be outlined for a student to do. The materials to be studied and the work to be done relate, naturally, to specific skills. These particular skills should be clearly set forth in the curriculum guide, since they are important goals of the level. Instead of thinking of a level as defined by certain instructional materials which a student would use, we might think of it solely in terms of the particular skills that would be studied. Logically, it might seem as though the content of a level should be defined by a list of the skills to be accomplished, but in practice it has proved to be too bulky to enter a long list of skills for each level in each subject on students' record sheets. There are other problems, too — these are discussed in Chapter Six. It is easier and more concise just to record that a child has completed a certain section of the instructional materials, and to have this imply that he has demonstrated satisfactory performance of certain skills.

## The Content Subjects

Judging from descriptions of nongraded programs that have appeared in brochures published by school systems and in journal articles, the curriculum in the content areas of social studies and science has generally not been divided into levels through which children could progress at varying rates. There are several reasons why nongraded schools have not done this. Two will be mentioned here; but first it should be said that it would be possible to organize the content subjects according to a levels plan if this was desired. A school system could list the main topics for each subject to be studied in each succeeding year, just as is done in many graded schools. Each topic might be divided into several sections. Individuals or small groups could progress at varying rates through sections of a given topic and on into different topics. If this plan was followed, the various children in a classroom would soon be working on different sections and different topics.

One reason why the levels plan has not been used with the content subjects is that many educators believe that there is value in having at least part of the day devoted to activities in which the whole class works on a common topic or enterprise. It is felt that such work provides opportunities for additional socializing experiences, for the development of group loyalty and social-mindedness, and for additional ways to motivate children. Also, if the work in the skill subjects is conducted so that the entire class is not working on the same skills at the same time, variety from this approach to instruction can be provided by having everyone study one or two common topics during part of the day. Variety in instructional procedures is regarded by many educators as desirable.

A second reason for not using levels with the content subjects is that in the elementary school, it *is* possible for children of diverse abilities to work together on a social studies or science topic, whereas it is probably more difficult for children of diverse abilities to work together on one of the skill subjects. To study and practice a particular skill requires that children should have reached a certain degree of readiness consisting of the ability to perform various lower level skills. Those of diverse abilities would not all achieve the necessary readiness. In one of the content subjects, however, pupils of different abilities could study a particular topic (such as food) together. Children of greater ability would be able to deal with some of the more complicated concepts and probably have greater insight regarding various interrelationships. They would probably read more extensively, use books that discussed the topic in greater depth, and could be expected to engage in more self-directed study while the teacher worked more directly with the pupils of lower ability.

The children who performed less well would probably not be able to study the topic in as much depth, but would be able to deal with some of the simpler concepts. They would probably read less extensively on their own and would use books written in simpler language and having more pictures. Obviously, an adequate assortment of reading materials on various levels of difficulty would be essential. The films, resource persons, fieldtrips, stories read by the teacher, and class discussions would certainly be important learning media for some of the slower children. Each child, whether of higher or lower performance, would take from the study the information, understandings, and insights that were meaningful to *him*, and in this way he would be having some measure of success at his own level.

If the program can be conducted so that it is acceptable for different pupils to vary in their depth of performance as they study a particular social studies or science topic, and if a reporting system can be devised which does not penalize those who work in a simpler manner, then the program can be considered nongraded in spirit. It is possible, therefore, to introduce the nongraded approach in the content subjects even though a levels plan is not used. The mere fact that certain topics in the content areas of the curriculum are specified for study during a given year does not in itself create a graded program. The crucial factor is how a teacher and school system envision the handling of work on a particular topic. As long as it is acceptable for different children in the same classroom to study a topic in different degrees of depth, the spirit of nongrading is being practiced.

Just because a sequence of topics is established in social studies or science,* it should not be inferred that each topic in the list is intrinsically more difficult than its predecessor. It is quite possible, though, to have this impression, because in the skill subjects the topics for study (levels) are arranged sequentially according to difficulty. If in social studies the topics themselves are not each more difficult than the last, how is it possible to have a curriculum in the content subjects that progresses longitudinally from simpler to more complex understandings? Such a program is possible, but it results from factors other than the particular topics chosen for study or the order in which they appear in the curriculum.

The topics themselves are not really of particular importance — they serve mainly as _vehicles_ for important learnings. For instance, the topics are a means by which significant understandings about the social and scientific world can be discovered, investigated, and analyzed. These understandings, and the thinking processes that are practiced as the children grapple with them, are important elements in the instructional program in the content subjects. In a social studies unit on the fire department, for instance, it is not this topic per se, nor specific information about the fire department which constitute important learnings. Instead, the vital elements are the deeper insights which are acquired regarding the basic social activities of man — such social activities as conserving and protecting, educating, organizing and governing, communicating, and producing. The study of the fire department, or any one of many other social studies topics, serves as a vehicle to help boys and girls gain more profound learnings and understandings about man's basic social activities.†

Most any broad topic in social studies or science can be conducted in the elementary school so that a variety of important understandings are considered — ranging from the simple to the more complex. One child may be ready to deal only with simple concepts. However, by the next unit, the understandings he gained at his own level in the last study may make it possible for him to grasp concepts which are a little more involved. A different child may have been ready to grasp more difficult understandings in the

---

*A sample list of social studies topics for the primary years appears in Chapter Five in the section entitled Diagram 4.

†The study of a particular topic also serves as a vehicle to provide other valuable learning experiences, such as practicing research and study skills, using the 3 R's and various democratic procedures in a functional manner, developing problem solving ability, and engaging in various expressional activities.

first unit. He will probably be ready to deal with them on a higher level by the time he works with them again in a later unit. Thus each child, depending on his readiness, fashions his own progression from simple to more complex understandings.

A teacher conducting a unit in one of the first or second year classrooms in a primary program would introduce the children to a range of understandings that would be on a somewhat easier level than the range with which a third or fourth year teacher might deal. There would, however, be considerable overlap, especially for adjacent years.

It is the understandings, not the topics, that should be viewed longitudinally. Attempts have been made to identify important understandings in social studies and science, and to arrange these in sequence. Such lists are available but since there is considerable debate regarding what the important understandings should be, the lists are rather tentative and none have received wide acceptance. Attempts have also been made to take a single broad understanding and break it down into smaller segments, some of which can be grasped before others. But here again, so many alternatives exist that no one list is likely to be widely adopted. Nevertheless, one or more of these lists should be available for every teacher, and major unit studies should be conducted so that pupils are helped to gain insight into important understandings.

It would be possible to take one of these lists and develop an entire course of self-instructional materials in a content subject, and then each child could progress at his own rate through them to acquire the desired understandings. But as indicated earlier, many educators have felt that there were reasons in favor of boys and girls doing some of their school work, especially in social studies and science, in whole-class projects.

Although an important part of the work in the content subjects might be conducted as whole-class projects, attention should be given to encouraging certain children to investigate special topics of interest. Through conferences with the teacher, these students could be helped to plan individual or pupil-team studies. The activities would probably be of short duration for primary children, but when older they could enjoy investigating a topic in greater depth and for a longer time. Some schools have found that certain elementary school students can engage in interesting and productive independent studies, especially when they have the resources of a well-equipped *learning materials center*. The need for such a center must be stressed, for unless children have learning materials to work with, they will be very limited in what they can do. Supplementary books, picture files, slides and filmstrip sets, tape recordings, and equipment for science demonstrations should be available.

Although much of the work in social studies and science is generally considered content, there are important _skills_ which are related to these content areas and in which children should receive instruction. Included here would be skills in using maps and globes, and various work-study skills such as using an index, interpreting graphs, and identifying the main ideas in written material. The study and practice of these skills could be arranged in sequence according to levels of difficulty. If self-instructional materials were available, children could progress in their learning of these skills at varying rates. Schools could devise their own instructional materials or use those that are available commercially. Examples of the latter include several of the SRA learning laboratories, programed workbooks produced by Coronet Films, the Study Skills Library from Educational Development Laboratories, a workbook entitled _Using the Library_ published by Charles E. Merrill Books, and an inexpensive series of map skills workbooks distributed by American Education Publications. All of these materials are designed for use with children in the upper years of elementary school, with the exception of the series of map skills workbooks which extend from second to sixth grade.

## Criticisms of the Levels Plan

## Criticism I

Various criticisms have been made of the levels plan of curriculum organization. One that has been frequently expressed is that the plan is nothing more than a graded program in disguise. The critics reason that the levels represent hurdles just as grades do.

It is true, of course, that the levels are hurdles which children must complete, but there are other factors which make the plan different from a graded program. With grades, the usual procedure is that all pupils of a given age are expected to jump the hurdles in unison. In a levels plan, on the other hand, children of the same age would not be working on the same hurdles at the same time and would progress at different rates; the nature of the hurdles (content of a level) might also be varied for different individuals. Thus, there is a marked difference in these two plans — the levels plan is not a graded program in disguise.

## Criticism II

Another criticism often made of the levels plan is that it is nothing more than a system of inter-classroom achievement grouping. The critics point to nongraded programs, both elementary and secondary, where such plans are in operation and where children are carefully assigned in such a way as to try to reduce the range of achievement levels with which any one teacher has to work. If a teacher in this type of program works with pupils who are assigned to him in a whole-class, lockstep manner, then the levels plan is basically no more than a system of inter-classroom achievement grouping. There are schools with this type of program; they are *partially nongraded.** In a _thoroughly nongraded_ program, however, each teacher would provide multi-level instruction for the range of levels that would still exist even after the attempt to form more homogeneous classes. In this case the levels plan would be something more than just a system of inter-classroom achievement grouping.

In considering this particular criticism, it is also important to remember that the levels plan is used in many nongraded programs where inter-classroom achievement grouping is not practiced — for instance, in self-contained, heterogeneous classes (see Chapter Five, section entitled Diagram 1). Practiced in this manner, the plan is obviously something more than just a system of inter-classroom achievement grouping.

## Criticism III

A third criticism is that the levels plan does not provide adequately for individual differences. This is so, say the critics, because

---

*Descriptions of this type of nongraded program appear in two places in Chapter Five: in the section entitled Diagram 3, and in the section on Team Teaching and Departmentalization.

each child is expected eventually to progress through the same levels, and thus the material to be learned is the same for all. The only differences that are provided for are differences in rate. Should there not also be provision for variations in content?

It is true that the levels plans in most nongraded schools focus primarily on providing variations in rate. This focus exists, however, not because of a limitation in the levels plan itself, but rather in the way it has been operated in most schools. There is nothing in the plan itself which precludes variations in the content. It should also be pointed out that in some instances, persons expressing this criticism seem to overlook entirely the fact that there *is* value in providing variations in rate. This type of variation helps to correct one major weakness of traditional practice in graded schools.

It is entirely possible for a levels plan also to embrace variations in content. The principal way to do this would be to have the less capable children study only the simpler elements of the work at a given level, and to enrich the work at that same level for students of greater ability. The enrichment might include learning supplementary skills and studying the basic skills in greater depth. A report card could be devised to show the work a child was doing. It would show the level he had achieved, and by means of several symbols would indicate whether there had been enrichment or whether the work was being done in a simpler manner.*

Teachers might be left entirely on their own to devise and carry out variations in the content of specific levels. With imaginative teachers who were willing to devote unusual amounts of time to their work, a desirable program geared to the needs of individual children would surely evolve. However, for a great many it would be too demanding for them to rely entirely on their own resources — they would want a more definite structure to guide them. The school's curriculum guide, in addition to listing the basic content for each level, could indicate ways in which the work of a specific level could be trimmed and presented in its simplest form, or enriched through study in greater depth or through study of additional items. It would be necessary, of course, for teachers to be provided with the instructional materials necessary to conduct these suggested variations.

Of the major skill subjects, reading is the one in which teachers have done the most to vary the content for different pupils. For

---

*See sample report form in Chapter Six.

instance, as a teacher discusses a story in the basal reader with the more able children, he can do so in a manner that requires greater understanding and insight from them. When those who are less capable arrive at the level that includes this same story, the teacher may conduct learning activities which focus more on a literal understanding of the events in the story. When individualized reading is part of the overall reading program, further opportunities for variations in content become available. Some of the books selected by the more able pupils are likely to require greater depth of understanding than the stories other children choose. The way the teacher conducts the individual conference can be adjusted for different individuals. A variety of independent work activities is another way learning experiences can be diversified. Self-instructional materials, as one example of an independent activity, could be used by certain children to study additional aspects of basic topics in the curriculum, or these materials might also be used to study a topic which was not a part of the basic curriculum.

To summarize the analysis of this criticism, it is important to realize that a levels plan can provide for variations in both rate and content. Thus when one pictures a series of levels through which children progress at varying rates, the content of each level would not have to be exactly the same for each child.

## Criticism IV

A further criticism of the levels plan is that it is pre-planned. The critics contend that this is undesirable because it reduces opportunities for learning based on emerging situations. Learning centered around emerging situations is thought to be valuable because (a) it often creates greater interest among the children, (b) it may help to develop self-reliance and social-mindedness, and (c) it provides opportunities for creative and imaginative thinking. Because learning of this type is often related to children's personal concerns in daily living, it can be especially meaningful.

The criticism that a levels system involves predetermined content is tied to an older controversy which existed long before the system became known — namely, whether curriculum should be pre-planned or emergent. In most elementary schools across America there has been a heavy emphasis on a pre-planned program. Advocates of Progressive Education have denounced this emphasis and argued for a curriculum that would encourage more emergent learning situations. In recent years, curriculum has been considerably influenced by suggestions from specialists in the separate disciplines. Generally, the suggestions of these specialists have been such that an extensively pre-planned program would be required rather than one which involved many emergent learning situations.

The very existence of a levels plan means that the curriculum has been pre-planned, at least to a certain degree, for a given level identifies certain skills that are to be learned. Thus, the possibility of a completely emergent program has been precluded. But few educators would argue in favor of a program that was completely emergent. Also, many teachers would have great difficulty in being successful at conducting a program of this type. Most educators believe that pre-planning of the curriculum is necessary; they differ only in the amount and the kind that is desirable. Since levels plans can differ in the amount and kind of pre-planning that is involved, many educators find the scheme an acceptable one.

The following illustration is presented to show that teachers can adhere rigidly to the content outlined for a specific level, or they can proceed in a manner which provides opportunities for emergent learning experiences. In many schools where a levels plan has been developed in reading, the levels have been identified by the names of the readers in the basic series. In one system the tenth level is designated by the book *More Friends Old and New*. If teachers were expected to adhere closely to the pre-planned curriculum, children who reached level ten might be required to do each activity set forth in the curriculum guide for this level. This might involve reading all of the stories called for in the guide, discussing the stories according to the outlines in the manual, and doing individualized, self-instruction practice work exactly as specified in the guide.

In another school, however, the program might be conducted differently. A teacher would be free to do whatever he felt was necessary to help children arrive at the point of being able to read material that was equivalent to stories in *More Friends Old and New*, or he might have the children read only a few stories in the reader but make considerable use of supplementary readers and/or trade books. A combination of sub-group instruction and individualized reading could be utilized. Certain pupils might make considerable use of individualized self-instruction materials whereas others would do less. The teacher could plan the work for the pupils, or involve them in setting sub-goals and exploring ways to reach these goals. This type of program would give rise to various emergent learning situations. A school's curriculum guide, which accompanied specific levels, might suggest ways for the teacher to initiate activities which would necessitate teacher-pupil planning and lead to emergent learning experiences.

Commercial materials for self-instruction, such as programed learning and the SRA learning laboratories, provide very few opportunities for emergent learning situations. If these materials are to be used in a nongraded program (and there would seem to be good reason to do so) activities which provide opportunities for emergent learning experiences will need to be provided in other ways. As indicated in the preceding paragraph, the teacher could help children in small-group work or through independent study to engage in emergent learning experiences. Particularly rich possibilities for learning based on emerging concerns would of course exist in other areas of the curriculum such as social studies, problems of classroom and school living, and science.

The critics who complain that a levels system is pre-planned also contend that this pre-arrangement prevents the program from adequately meeting the needs of children, because there are so many unknown differences that it would be impossible to anticipate them all in the pre-planning. It is certainly true that the varying needs cannot be completely anticipated. But is this reason to abandon pre-planning? Many educators see the need of a compromise. Certain elements of each level can be planned in advance, but the teacher can be given considerable latitude to modify these elements and to determine day-to-day procedures in light of children's unfolding needs.

The analysis presented in this section has attempted to show that although a levels plan of curriculum organization necessitates pre-planning, this need not completely eliminate from the school program emergent learning situations and variations to provide for unexpected differences in children. Whether these latter practices occupy an important place in the instructional program, or a minor one, depends on various factors, but use of a levels plan need not be one of them.

## Criticism V

It has been said by critics that the levels plan may deter teachers from conducting a daily program in which there are opportunities for the integration of work in the skill subjects and the content areas. Since two types of integrating activities are involved here, the analysis of this criticism consists of two parts.

(1) There appears to be nothing in the levels plan for the skill subjects that would interfere with a teacher's effort to conduct broad studies in science, social studies, and problems of living so that children had opportunities to make functional use of the basic skills. The problems teachers would have in providing integrating experiences of this type would not seem to be greater whether the instruction in the basic skills involved a levels plan or was conducted on a single level as is often done in the typical graded school.

(2) A second type of integrating activity involves conducting social studies and science units in such a way that pupils will experience a need to improve various skills in reading, numbers, and writing. The teacher is then expected to provide opportunities for learning and practicing the needed skills. If children were already doing work at their own levels in a multi-level program of instruction in the skill subjects, it might be difficult to find additional time in the school day to devote to the particular skills for which the unit activities had created a need.

It might seem as though the use of the levels plan was the culprit here, standing in the way of more attention being given to the integration of learnings, but the hindrance really results from two other factors. The first factor is whether or not there is a program of instruction in the skill subjects which is _separate_ from the children's work in the content areas. If there is, it is this fact which is important and not whether the separate program is organized by levels. Merely changing to single-level instruction but maintaining the separate program would not result in any greater opportunities for the integration of learnings. The very fact that there is a lack of this type of integration in most graded schools where both a separate program and single-level instruction exist, would confirm this.

A second factor standing in the way of more attention being given to this type of integrating activity is the _degree_ to which the separate program in the skill subjects has been pre-planned. If it is extensively pre-arranged with detailed descriptions of exactly what should be taught in each subject, and teachers are expected to follow this program closely, then they are likely to consume so much time and effort in trying to carry out the program that they would probably not get around to having the children study the particular skills for which unit activities might have created a need.

In most schools, whether nongraded or graded, the program of instruction in the basic skills is separate, at least in part, from the work the boys and girls are expected to do in the content areas. However, in some systems an attempt has been made to de-emphasize this separation by encouraging teachers to take time from the pre-planned program in skills to work on other skills as the need for them is generated by unit studies. If much is to come of this, the administrative staff would have to make it clear that it would not be necessary for children to work every day or every week on the pre-planned program of skills. In other words, teachers should be encouraged not to devote all of their time and energy in skills teaching to the pre-planned, separate program. To convince teachers of the sincerity of this pronouncement, the pre-planned program of work in the basic skills would need to be broadly defined rather than to list too many specifics. As soon as the program became too specific, many teachers would probably feel compelled to follow it closely so that pupils would not "miss" any of it. It appears then that the levels plan itself need not be a hindrance in conducting a program in which an effort is made to integrate work in the basic skills and the content areas.

## Criticism VI

A sixth criticism is that the levels plan in nongraded schools will result in too much attention being placed on the skill subjects and a de-emphasis of other parts of the curriculum, especially social studies and science. The critics suggest that many elementary teachers are already committed to a program that places reading and arithmetic at the top of the list of priorities. If teachers are now required to teach these subjects by means of multi-level instruction, which is more difficult than whole-class, single-level instruction, so much effort will be required that the teacher will have little time or energy left to do an adequate job of teaching other parts of the curriculum. The critics also suggest that since the levels plan is generally applied to the skill subjects and not to the content subjects, the newness of the program in the skill areas will cause teachers to focus attention there rather than on other parts of the program where instructional procedures are not so different.

These dangers are indeed real, but not insurmountable. Proper safeguards are needed to help keep a desired balance in the daily program. In many schools, teachers are given a guide to the amount of time to be allocated to each of the curriculum areas. They should be helped to understand that they are to operate within the spirit of these allocations. Supervisors will have to work with them to keep them from devoting more than the allotted time to reading and arithmetic, even though certain teachers may feel they could produce better results in these subjects by giving more time to them. Only in this way can time be kept available for other important areas of the curriculum. Extra efforts would also have to be made to help teachers conduct social studies and science programs which were adequate. Additional teaching materials could be secured, and by means of workshops or supervisory assistance, teachers could be helped to plan and conduct meaningful activities in the content areas.

During the several years in which multi-level instruction is being introduced in the skill areas, it would certainly be difficult to balance all aspects of the curriculum in a desired manner. But perhaps this is not too high a price to pay to obtain the advantages of nongrading. With proper leadership from the supervisory staff, a reasonable balance should be possible in time.

## Summary

The purpose of this chapter has been two-fold: to explain the levels plan of curriculum organization in nongraded schools, and to discuss several criticisms that have been made of this plan. The levels plan is a means to facilitate nongrading. It has usually been confined to work in the skill subjects. The curriculum in each skill subject is broken down into segments which are called levels. The teacher attempts to help the children who are assigned to him work at the different levels for which they are ready and to progress at their own rates to more advanced levels. If a teacher is conducting a thoroughly nongraded program, instruction in a given subject would be carried on at different levels at the same time; this is referred to as multi-level teaching. The average child would be able to complete several levels in a subject in a year's time.

The plan has not been used very often to facilitate nongrading in the content subjects of social studies and science. Study of the same topic by the whole-class has continued as the dominant practice. It is quite possible, however, to conduct this type of program in a nongraded manner. Various children can study the topic in different degrees of depth. If the differences in individual performance are accepted by the teacher and other school personnel, and if the reporting system does not penalize the children who deal mainly with simpler concepts and understandings, the spirit of nongrading will prevail.

Various criticisms have been directed at the levels plan. Six of these were discussed in this chapter. An analysis of these criticisms suggests that some are based on misunderstanding whereas others involve problems which with care can probably be at least partially solved. The levels plan seems to be sufficiently flexible so that it can be modified by the staff in a school system to satisfy local needs. For this reason the plan has been found to be a workable one in many nongraded schools.

# 5

# Assigning Children to Teachers in Nongraded Schools

## Introduction

It has been this author's experience in talking with teachers and administrators about nongrading that they have many questions about the ways a nongraded program might actually function. Two questions seem to be of particular concern: How are children assigned to teachers? and how would children progress from year to year, and from one teacher to another?

In this chapter an attempt is made to answer these questions. Diagrams are presented to show how children might move through nongraded programs that involve different schemes for assigning children to teachers.

It will be recalled from Chapter One that there are three principal plans for implementing a nongraded program. Each involves a different scheme for assigning children to teachers. In Plan 1 children are placed in self-contained classes according to age, and are heterogeneous in terms of academic performance. Diagram 1, presented later in this chapter, illustrates how children would move through this type of nongraded program.

In Plan 2, children are placed in self-contained classes according to performance levels, and instruction is provided from one class to the next on different levels of difficulty. In this way inter-classroom achievement grouping is practiced. Diagrams 2 and 3 in this chapter illustrate different ways this plan might function when the children in a given classroom are approximately the same age. Diagrams 4 and 5 illustrate the same programs when the children in a given classroom are of mixed-ages.

In the third plan for implementing a nongraded program, a large aggregation of children is regrouped from time to time during the day or week to form clusters or classes that work on different levels under the direction of different teachers. This plan could be conducted as either a departmentalized program or one involving team teaching. An explanation is given of how team teaching arrangements could be introduced in Diagrams 1, 2, 3, 4, and 5. Nongraded, departmentalized programs are also explained briefly.

The five diagrams plus the examples of team teaching and departmentalization which are presented represent the principal ways nongraded programs have been conducted. After studying many nongraded schools, it is this writer's belief that each approximates one or the other of the examples presented here. The fact that a description of each of the major variations is presented here in one place is an important feature of this book. Many teachers and administrators who have read or heard about one type of nongraded program have wondered whether there were other ways the program could be conducted. There are a number of ways, and the major ones are presented here.

The reader is cautioned not to regard the examples as exact blueprints. Variations and combinations of these plans would be desirable. Local conditions would surely necessitate that variations be made.

The five diagrams are preceded by Diagram G which illustrates a graded primary program. Diagram G is included so that pupils' progress through a graded school can be compared with the way they proceed through nongraded programs. Since all of the diagrams show the same aggregation of fifty to sixty children starting in kindergarten and progressing year by year, the way a given child is assigned to classrooms in one plan can be compared with his placement in other plans.

Each of the diagrams shows only the primary years of the elementary school. The reason for this limitation is that the inclusion of the upper elementary years would have made the diagrams more bulky and thus perhaps more confusing to interpret. The procedures which are involved can be displayed as well by a diagram confined to the primary years as one which extends into the upper years.

Although the diagrams do not show the later years in the elementary school, this should not be interpreted to mean that nongrading is not a desirable approach with older children. It is just as desirable for these pupils — really it is more so — because as they grow older the range of differences increases. If nongrading is practiced only during the primary years, this is likely to produce problems when the boys and girls progress to the upper grades. Pupils entering fourth grade will vary considerably in performance levels and will be working at different places in the instructional materials. Because of this, it would be difficult for a fourth grade teacher to conduct a graded program. The situation that would exist would suggest that the work in the later years should also be ungraded.

Since the diagrams presented in this chapter are limited to the primary years, the beginning of fourth grade has been considered as a "cut-off point". An assumption is made that the nongraded programs do not extend into the upper years of the elementary school and that children would remain in the primary unit until they were as ready as possible for fourth grade, although they would not be kept there more than two years beyond the usual time. If the entire elementary program was nongraded, a school staff might prefer not to have a formal barrier midway through the program. There would, of course, be a hurdle at the end of the elementary years when children would be confronted with the entrance standards of the junior high school.

## Diagram G

### A Graded School and Heterogeneous Grouping

Diagram G represents a graded program that is combined with an arrangement for heterogeneous classes. The children in a given self-contained classroom are approximately the same chronological

| | 1st year | 2nd year — for | 3rd year — for | 4th year — for | Beginning of 4th Grade |
|---|---|---|---|---|---|
| | Kindergarten | most children | most children | most children | |

Fall ⟶ Spring

| | | F | | Sp | F | | Sp | F | | Sp | |
|---|---|---|---|---|---|---|---|---|---|---|---|

A.M. Level 1

| F | | Sp |
|---|---|---|
| 2 3 4 5 6 | into 7 | |
| 2 3 4 5 6 | 7 | |
| 2 3 4 5 6 7 | 8 | |

| F | | Sp |
|---|---|---|
| 8 | 9 | into 10 |
| 9 | | 10 |
| 9 | 10 | 11 |

| F | | Sp |
|---|---|---|
| 11 | 12 | into 13 |
| 12 | | 13 |
| 12 | 13 | 14 |

P.M. Level 1

| F | | Sp |
|---|---|---|
| 2 3 4 5 6 | into 7 | |
| 2 3 4 5 6 | 7 | |
| 2 3 4 5 6 7 | 8 | |

| F | | Sp |
|---|---|---|
| 8 | 9 | into 10 |
| 9 | | 10 |
| 9 | 10 | 11 |

| F | | Sp |
|---|---|---|
| 11 | 12 | into 13 |
| 12 | | 13 |
| 12 | 13 | 14 |

**DIAGRAM G**

age, except for those who are _repeating_ or who have been _double promoted_. Since heterogeneous grouping has been employed, the full range of achievement levels would be represented in each classroom. Diagram G shows two classrooms at each grade level for a total of eight classrooms in the kindergarten through third grade primary unit. The same number of classrooms is also used in each of the illustrations of nongraded programs. There are approximately twenty-five to thirty children in each room in all of the diagrams.

Although there is a wide range in the achievement levels in a given classroom, the theory of the graded plan dictates that all of the children study only the skills, topics, and textbooks designated for the grade and complete them in a year's time. In reading, for instance, all of the pupils in second grade would be expected to complete the work identified by numbers 9 and 10. Level 9 consists of part one of the second-grade reader in the basal series, and level 10 is part two of the second-grade reader.

In this and later diagrams, only the work in reading has been shown. The achievement levels for a different subject could have been used instead. Levels for several subjects could be shown together in one diagram, but the diagram would be so cluttered that it would be difficult to interpret. The reader will have to imagine a series of diagrams, one showing achievement levels for each skill subject.

The complete reading program might consist of the following levels:

| | |
|---|---|
| 1 general readiness | 10 second reader, part two |
| 2 readiness book | 11 transition reader |
| 3 first pre-primer | 12 third reader, part one |
| 4 second pre-primer | 13 third reader, part two |
| 5 third pre-primer | 14 transition reader |
| 6 primer | 15 fourth reader, part one |
| 7 first reader | 16 fourth reader, part two |
| 8 transition reader | 17 advanced reading |
| 9 second reader, part one | 18 more advanced reading |

The levels which represent transition readers are not always included in the diagrams because teachers often do not have all children use these books. Some pupils skip them and begin with the next reader.

Diagram G shows that the teacher in each classroom has formed three sub-groups for reading instruction. Looking from left to right in the diagram for a given room, we see an approximate representation of how the children in each sub-group would progress from fall to spring through the reading levels specified for a given grade.

In a program that was rigidly graded, the children in a given class would do only the reading outlined for that grade, no more and no less. For example, in the second grade, they would all begin with level 8 or 9 regardless of the fact that some would probably be able to read more difficult material. As the year progressed, no-one would be allowed to go ahead into level 12, for this is work reserved for the next year. Children who were not ready for level 8 at the beginning of the second grade, would have been retained in the grade below, or if promoted in the hope of catching up, would be pushed through the second grade materials regardless of readiness. Some of the pupils in the latter category might fail in their attempt to do the second grade work. In this case, they would have to repeat, that is, do the work over again the next year.

Instruction in the other subjects would be similar to reading. At each grade level all the children in the grade would be expected to "cover" the same material in a year's time. Rather than use sub-groups as in reading, however, teachers would probably conduct whole-class instruction in the other subjects.

## Diagram 1
## A Nongraded School and Heterogeneous Grouping

Diagram 1 illustrates a nongraded program that has been combined with a plan for heterogeneous grouping.[1] The grade labels have now been dropped, and therefore the only way to compare Diagram 1 with Diagram G is to match years in the four-year primary unit. Most children would take four years to progress through Diagram 1, but some would require an extra year or two while a few might need only three years. Examples will be presented later to show how these children would be assigned to classrooms.

As in all of the plans, there are two classrooms for each year in the four-year sequence. The children in each self-contained class-

---

[1]Diagram 1 illustrates Plan 1 of the three principal plans for implementing a nongraded program.

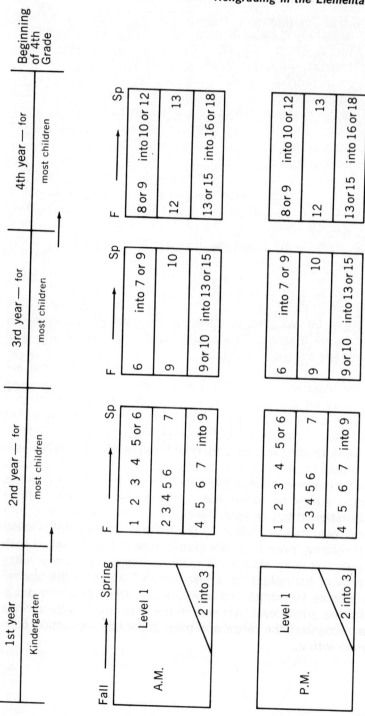

DIAGRAM 1

room are approximately the same chronological age. These are *single-age* classrooms. Exceptions to this will be discussed later.

Since heterogeneous grouping is part of Diagram 1, the children in each classroom will differ widely in achievement. As the teacher conducts a nongraded program, he attempts to work with individuals or small groups at their own level of achievement — thus allowing different pupils to do different work. Some will be studying more advanced materials while others proceed at a slower pace. There is no expectation that all pupils in a specific class would complete the same work in a year's time.

Diagram 1 shows that in a given classroom a wider range of reading levels would be studied than was the case in Diagram G. For instance, in a room where an average pupil was in his third year, the reading levels in the fall of the year might range from 6 to 10. For instructional purposes, the teacher might think of these children as being in three sub-groups, as indicated on the diagram. During the course of the year the slower pupils might progress from level 6 to 7 or 8, while the more advanced might begin at level 10 and proceed into 15. For their next year, those who are slower might be assigned to either of the rooms immediately to the right in the diagram. They would begin in the fall at the level where they left off in the spring.

The levels indicated on the diagram for a given classroom are merely for illustrative purposes and should not be interpreted as setting limits on the levels that could be studied. It is important that this be understood. At the beginning of the school year, the teacher in each classroom would assess where his particular children were in reading and start them at these levels. During the year he would take them as far as they could go. The levels where pupils in a given classroom started and ended would depend on the pupils and would surely be somewhat different for the next class of students assigned to that room.

It may seem that in Diagram 1 the teacher is faced with a wider range of reading levels than in a graded school. But the *actual* span of children's reading abilities is really the same in corresponding classrooms of both plans. It is just that in Diagram G the teacher merely ignores the range and provides only the instruction designated for the grade level. Whereas in the nongraded classroom the teacher recognizes the range and tries to provide instruction commensurate with it.

Although Diagram 1 and the others which follow indicate that three sub-groups might be formed in each classroom, there is nothing in the nongraded approach which demands this. A teacher might have four, or two, or no sub-groups. If the latter, the work would have to consist entirely of individualized instruction. Instead of conducting a program which involved only one method of teaching, many would prefer a combination approach consisting of both sub-group and individualized instruction.

In a combination approach a teacher might have the sub-groups meet frequently, or only occasionally, depending on his particular wishes. Membership in the groups might be continuing and based on general reading ability, or the groups could be re-formed from time to time according to particular needs of the children. In the latter case, groups might be formed on the basis of common weakness in a particular skill, common interest among pupils, or need for a certain method of instruction such as one emphasizing audio rather than visual learning exercises.

Just because the work in the skill subjects is organized by levels, this does not mean that all children who are studying at approximately the same level must be brought together in a sub-group for instruction. Some teachers might do this, but others might make less use of this procedure and instead rely more on different forms of individualized instruction. The reader will find additional comments in Chapter Four about the various teaching methods that could be used in a multi-level instructional program.

The sub-groups are indicated on the diagrams only because this is a convenient way to show the range of reading levels in a classroom at any given moment, as well as how children of different abilities might progress from fall to spring and from year to year. The latter is an important feature of the diagrams. It is possible to follow a given child as he progresses from one level to another through the several years of the primary program. The reader can then look at other diagrams and follow the same child when his room assignment is handled differently.

Although each level in the diagrams consists of one of the readers in the basal series, this particular way of identifying the content of a level is not essential to nongrading. The work of a specific level could consist of something else; anything a particular school staff decided upon. Each level might involve a series of sections from a set of individualized self-instruction workbooks. If the language experience approach was being used as the method of teaching beginning reading, appropriate activities could be identified as the content of different levels.[2] As pupils in such a program moved into individualized reading, the work for each level would involve reading a variety of books and practicing skills as needed. Since children in a program of individualized reading are usually encouraged to select the books they want to read, the content for particular levels would not be specifically defined. Because of this indefiniteness, it would be difficult to determine the level at which an individual was working. To gain an approximate indication of a child's reading level, the teacher could have him read briefly from several different books in a basal series. Whichever book the teacher and child decided was "just about right", would be the level used for reporting purposes. Admittedly, this would be only a rough measure, but viewed over a period of several years, this system would provide an approximate indication of progress from one level of difficulty to the next.

Teachers and administrators who are considering a nongraded program will surely have questions about the fate of boys and girls who make unusually slow progress. What happens to these students? Using a third-year classroom as an example, the slower children might have reached level 7 or 8 by the end of the year. For their next year, they could be placed in either one of the fourth-year classrooms to continue at their own level, or they could be placed in a third-year room where their work level would not be too different from that of some of the children in that room. The latter assignment might be made if the teacher felt that a child would need an extra year in the nongraded primary instead of the usual four. The child would be a year older than most of the others in the classroom, but he would not "repeat" any of the reading work. He would proceed in reading at the level where he left off in the spring.

A slow child might spend his extra year in the kindergarten or any one of the other classrooms; the staff would have to decide

---

[2]One example of a progression of activities for the language experience approach is presented by Jeannette Veatch. She cautions, however, that there will be some children who will not advance in exactly this order. "(1) Getting to know people, (2) Creative expression and talking, (3) Seeing, writing, and hearing our own words, (4) Moving into sentence recognition, (5) Reading our own sentences, (6) Early level word perception, (7) Moving into word analysis, (8) Word analysis, and (9) Word analysis again becomes word perception." Reading easy books is a part of the experiences for the last three levels. Jeannette Veatch, *Reading in the Elementary School* (New York: The Ronald Press Company, 1966), p. 209. Chapters viii and xi in this book contain a helpful discussion of the way children progress in a program involving the language experience approach followed by individualized reading.

what was best for the individual. Pupils who demonstrated during their first year in the primary unit that they were especially immature should probably spend an extra year in a first-year classroom. Some "slow starters" in reading could be moved along with their age-mates if it was believed that they might eventually make more rapid progress. When a child spends an extra year in the primary unit, his number of years in the program would no longer correspond to the guideline which appears across the top of the diagram. This guideline applies only to children who take four years to progress through the primary unit.

A child's reading achievement should not be the sole criterion of whether he spent an extra year in the primary unit. His social and emotional maturity would be important considerations, as well as his level of progress in other areas of work. It should not be expected that all slower students, even after spending this extra time in the program, will match the other children in terms of quality of performance. A nongraded program will not eliminate the fact that they perform on a lower level in certain areas, but it will give them more of an opportunity to have successful learning experiences on their own level.

A few children would be able to complete the primary unit in less than four years. A child who had advanced to level 12 or 13 by the middle of his third year might be moved to a fourth-year classroom where some of the members would also be working at these levels. At the end of the year, he would move into fourth grade, thus completing the primary unit in three years. He would not have "skipped" any work in reading, nor in any of the other skill subjects if they were also conducted in a nongraded manner.

Although the nongraded approach illustrated in Diagram 1 removes some of the difficulties associated with having a child spend an extra year in school, there is no way in this plan to camouflage the fact that such a child is now in a classroom with other pupils who are a year younger. This same problem exists in Diagrams 2 and 3 which also involve single-age classrooms. Parents, and through them their children, are likely to continue to regard such a child as one who has "failed" or who is "repeating". This way of thinking is a product of the graded school and is likely to persist as long as parents remember the graded plan. This is discouraging, but a reality that is likely to accompany the use of Diagram 1.

It is possible to gain the impression from the description of Diagram 1, and the descriptions of the other diagrams too, that the reassignment of children from one room to another would occur only after the end of each school year. Actually, however, the reassignment of an individual could occur at any time the staff felt that his learning environment could be improved. The practice of moving some of the boys and girls during the school year instead of at the end of the year, might also help children and parents break away from the habit of thinking only in terms of year-end promotion and retention policies, and all that they imply in graded schools.

Diagram 1 shows that a few children toward the end of their first year would be ready to begin to read. As they became ready, the teacher would help them with level 2, and possibly 3. Consistent with the nongraded approach, these children would be helped to move ahead into reading rather than be required to wait until the next year.

For teachers and administrators who desire to move gradually toward a nongraded program, reading is certainly the easiest of the skill subjects to ungrade. Many teachers already have their classes organized into reading groups. The next step is to abandon the policy of requiring that pupils in a given grade study only the materials designated for that grade. Teachers would conduct instruction in reading at whatever levels were appropriate for specific children. A next step might be to begin ungrading the arithmetic program by providing multi-level instruction. Later, spelling and handwriting could also be changed to multi-level teaching. As indicated in Chapter Four, the nongrading of work in the content subjects would be handled differently.

In Diagram 1, the children might have a different teacher each year during the four years of the nongraded primary. However, in a few schools that have programs similar to Diagram 1, teachers have been encouraged to remain with a given group of children for two years. This is referred to as *teacher-cycling*. Teacher-cycling is not unique in nongraded programs, for there are graded schools where this same procedure has been practiced.

Across the top of Diagram 1, and each of the other diagrams as well, there is a guideline which is divided into years. At various places in this chapter, reference is made to the guideline by identifying a particular classroom as a second-year room, a third-year room, and so forth. It would be a mistake for teachers and administrators to refer in public to a room by its _year_ designation. A room could be identified by the teacher's name, which would be posted on the classroom door and used in school notices.

## Diagram 2
## A Nongraded School and Partial Inter-Classroom Achievement Grouping

Diagram 2 illustrates a nongraded program that is coupled with *partial* inter-classroom achievement grouping.[3] The children in a given self-contained room are approximately the same chronological age, except for those who are spending five years in the primary unit or those who are taking only three years.

*Partial* achievement grouping differs from *full* achievement grouping in that only the extremes, the very slowest pupils and the unusually able, are separated. The placement of children according to reading performance begins the second year. As can be seen from the diagram, each classroom contains a considerable range of reading achievement levels, but the very slowest are not in the same classroom with the most advanced. The slowest children at each age level have been assigned to the classrooms in the top row.

In this diagram, as well as in the other nongraded programs explained in this chapter, the reader is cautioned not to consider the reading levels that are indicated for each classroom as fixed or unchanging. The partciular level that was highest or lowest in a given classroom would depend on the children in the class and not on a prior decision that only certain levels could be taught in that room.

In any program that involves homogeneous grouping, a criterion for grouping must be identified. In Diagram 2, general reading performance is the measure. A different criterion — such as arithmetic achievement, or a combination of several criteria — such as general school performance and mental age, might have been used. Whichever is used to assign children to different rooms in a program of inter-classroom achievement grouping, definite problems will be encountered. A brief discussion of these difficulties is presented in the description of Diagram 3. One problem, however, will be discussed here because there are better possibilities for coping with it in Diagram 2 than in Diagram 3.

Whenever an attempt is made to assign children to classrooms on the basis of ability or achievement, this is likely to give rise to such terms as *slow class* or *fast group*. Other terms, less suitable,

---

[3]Diagram 2 is an example of Plan 2 of the three principal plans for implementing a nongraded program.

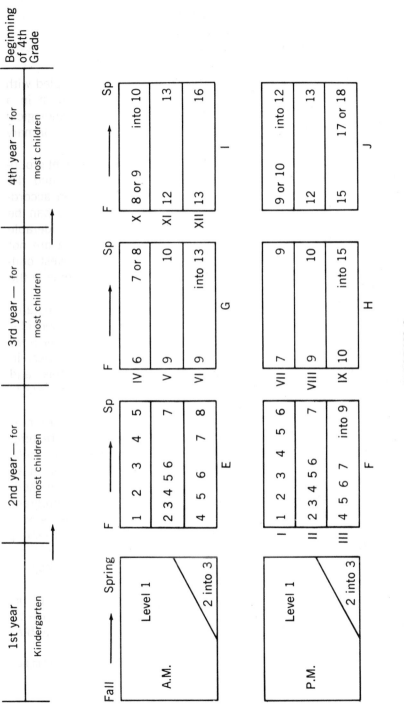

DIAGRAM 2

may also be applied by certain parents and children. It is difficult to camouflage this type of grouping practice although there are more opportunities for it in partial achievement grouping than in full achievement grouping. In the former, only a few are actually being assigned to one classroom or the other on the basis of achievement or ability. The fact that so few pupils are involved would result in fewer children and parents realizing the existence of the practice or being able to determine which classroom was which.

Further camouflage could be provided by shifting teachers from year to year so that no particular one was continuously identified with a faster or slower class. Another maneuver in Diagram 2 would be to take the large number of children whose reading levels overlap in the two classrooms for a given year, and intermix them from one year to the next. Thus, certain pupils of average performance would not always be destined to work with the slowest ones. At some time during the primary years, all of the average pupils would have opportunities to associate with both the least able and the most able.

In Diagram 2, alternate placements exist for many of the children. Many educators consider it desirable for a program to provide alternate placements for individual children. A child who does not do well in one class because his achievement level is too high or too low relative to the others there, or because of problems in getting along with certain classmates, or problems of working with a particular teacher, may find a more suitable learning environment in a different room. A comparison of the reading levels in the two classrooms for any given year will reveal that many children could be placed in one room as well as another. Many alternate placements exist. Only the very slowest and the most advanced would be destined for specific rooms, and even in these cases, alternate placements exist, for it would be possible to place a very slow child in a room with children a year younger, and to assign an unusually capable pupil to a room with children a year older.

Teacher-cycling could be practiced in Diagram 2 just as in Diagrams 1 and G. The staff in a school would need to weigh the advantages and disadvantages of this procedure, and then make its own decision whether or not to utilize this practice.

Diagram 2 is a compromise between Diagram 1, which has no achievement grouping, and Diagram 3, which involves full achievement grouping. Many educators believe there are definite advantages in having a classroom in which there is considerable diversity in interests and performance. A number of teachers, however, believe their daily teaching would be easier if there was less diversity. Diagram 2 might appeal to both parties, because the extremes in diversity of performance have been reduced, yet considerable variation remains.

# Diagram 3
## A Nongraded School and Full Inter-Classroom Achievement Grouping

Diagram 3 illustrates a nongraded program which is combined with a plan for full inter-classroom achievement grouping.[4] Most of the pupils in a given self-contained class are the same age. Room assignments are made by dividing all those of a given age into two groups according to reading achievement. The top half in reading is placed in one room and the lower half is assigned to the other room. This type of placement begins the second year. Instead of using just general reading achievement as the criterion for grouping, a standard based on the average of a child's performance in several areas could be used.

The levels indicated for a given classroom in the diagram are only suggestions. The levels would vary somewhat from year to year in a classroom, depending on the particular children assigned there.

Diagram 3 differs from Diagram 2 only in the degree to which inter-classroom achievement grouping has been effected. Maximum separation of achievement levels has been the goal. An attempt is made to place all of the more advanced readers in one room and all those making slower progress in the other room. There is a minimum of overlap in the reading levels of students in the two rooms, existing only among the middle or average achievers in reading. In Diagram 2, on the other hand, there was only a minimum separation of achievement levels. Only the very fastest and slowest in reading were assigned so that they would not be together in the same classroom. Because each of the two rooms for a given year still had a fairly wide range of reading levels, there was considerable overlap in the reading performance from one room to the other.

If there is limited overlap between the two classrooms for a given year, there would be fewer alternative placements for children,

---

[4]Diagram 3 is another example of Plan 2 of the three principal plans for implementing a nongraded program.

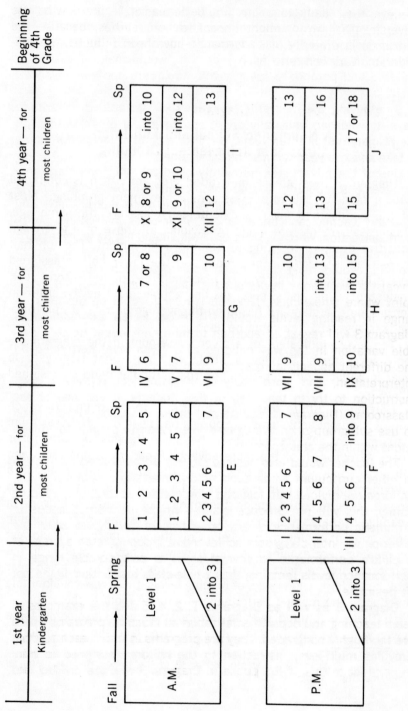

**DIAGRAM 3**

at least in terms of general reading performance. Most of the better readers would be together during their entire four years in the primary unit, while the less advanced readers would find themselves together in a classroom each year. This would make it easier for children and parents to identify the slow room and the advanced room.

By studying the diagram, the reader will be able to determine ways in which an unusually bright student could progress through the primary unit in three years. Ways for a child of low performance to take an extra year can also be ascertained.

One of the advantages frequently cited for full, inter-classroom achievement grouping is that instruction will be easier for the teacher. Supposedly, the children will be more nearly alike, and thus the teacher can conduct more whole-class instruction. Multi-level instruction, which is more difficult, should not be as necessary. Although many teachers wish that inter-classroom achievement grouping would make instruction easier, research studies clearly reveal that variations in performance levels are not reduced to the point where whole-class, lockstep teaching would be desirable. A range in reading levels would still exist, as an examination of Diagram 3 will reveal. In addition to this there would be considerable variation in the way children at a given level performed on the different aspects of reading, such as sight vocabulary, recall, interpretation, and word analysis. It would not represent good instruction to try to teach all of the students in any one of the classrooms (Diagram 3) the same lesson. A teacher would need to use sub-group or individualized instruction to provide for differences within the classroom.

The teacher would also need to provide differentiated instruction in other curriculum areas such as arithmetic and spelling. If the children are divided into fast and slow classes according to reading ability, this will not produce classes which are homogeneous in arithmetic performance or any other type of work. Even when the criterion for inter-classroom achievement grouping is an average of a child's performance in several areas, a considerable range in performance levels remains; thus whole-class instruction would not be desirable.

Diagram 3 as well as Diagrams 1, 2, 4, 5 and the examples of team teaching and departmentalization all illustrate programs which are *thoroughly* nongraded. They are programs in which each teacher provides multi-level instruction to the children assigned to him. In contrast to this, if the pupils in Diagram 3 who are divided into fast and slow classes were taught by the whole-class, lockstep method, then the school's program would be *partially* rather than *thoroughly* nongraded. It would be at least partially nongraded, however, because not all of the children of a given age would be expected to do the same thing at the same time. Those in classes in the top row of the diagram would not be expected to do the same work as their counterparts in the classes in the bottom row. A program of this type is one example of a multi-track plan. It also illustrates one of the ways to conduct Plan 2 of the three principal plans for implementing a nongraded program (see Chapter One).

Attempts at inter-classroom achievement grouping create various concerns and problems: (1) many teachers prefer not to be assigned to a slow classroom. (2) A number of educators believe that homogeneous grouping which involves relatively fixed groups continuing for a long period of time may have a negative effect on the self-concepts of children in the slow classroom, and cause pupils in the more advanced class to develop undesirable attitudes of superiority. (3) Certain educators believe that it is undemocratic to segregate children permanently on the basis of achievement and that students of varying abilities should have opportunities to associate with each other as they do their work. (4) Many persons in education believe that a diverse environment does more to enhance certain desirable human qualities than one in which the variables have been reduced. (5) Some parents would be likely to oppose the placement of their child in a "slow" classroom. In some cases the reasons for this opposition would be tenuous, but in other cases there might be sound educational reasons for the opposition.

Although numerous research studies have been conducted to determine whether children who were grouped homogeneously learned more than children not grouped in that manner, the results have been conflicting. At the present time, little support for this grouping scheme can be gained from the research that has been conducted.

More than likely some of the pupils in the slow classrooms would need an extra year in the primary unit. Such extra time might be spent in any one of the classrooms in the regular four-year sequence. They would be with children who were a year younger, which would continue to be the case for the rest of their years in the primary program. An alternative policy would be to have most of the children who needed an extra year wait to take it after the regular fourth year. Providing there was a sufficient number, a separate class could be formed for just these boys and girls. Hopefully the size of this class might not be too large, and pupils could receive more individual help before going on to fourth grade. It would probably be necessary to employ an extra teacher to conduct this class.

Children who spend an extra year in the primary unit would not need to repeat any work in the skill subjects in which the work had been ungraded. Of course, if reading was the only nongraded subject, there would be work to re-do in the other skill subjects. In the content areas it is likely that those who took an extra year would have to study science and social studies topics over again. This would be necessary if there was a standard sequence of prescribed topics. The repetition could be avoided, however, if there was a dual list of topics. Teachers, for instance, in the top tier of classrooms in Diagram 3 might follow one sequence of topics while the teachers in the bottom tier followed a different, but comparable, sequence. In schools where a dual list of topics was not used, a child could be assigned to a different teacher for his extra year. The new teacher would very likely conduct the work differently from the previous one, and this might result in the child's gaining deeper insights into important concepts rather than merely repeating his previous year's activities.

If all the children who were spending an extra year in the primary unit did so in a special classroom after the regular fourth year, it would not be necessary to repeat any topics in the content subjects, for different ones could be studied. Pupils who took only three years to complete the primary unit would skip certain topics in the standard four-year social studies and science curricula. However, because of their added maturity, these especially bright children might have acquired deeper insights and understandings regarding many social studies and science concepts, which awareness might compensate for having skipped the study of a few particular topics.

Diagram 3 represents an attempt to form classrooms in which there is considerable homogeneity in reading performance. In an effort to increase homogeneity, a variation of this plan has been tried in some schools. The variation results in mixed-age classes. Referring to Diagram 3, the pupils in room H who are at or near level 10 in the fall could be assigned instead to Room I, and the pupils at level 8 or 9 in Room I in the fall could be assigned instead to Room H. There would then be a smaller range in the reading levels in each room but each class would contain boys and girls of two ages. Diagram 5 shows the pupils assigned in the way just described. Both Diagrams 4 and 5 involve mixed-age classes.

## Diagram 4

### A Nongraded School and Mixed-Age Classes with Partial Inter-Classroom Achievement Grouping

This diagram illustrates a nongraded program that also includes arrangements for (1) mixed-age classes, and (2) partial inter-classroom achievement grouping.[5] Each class is a self-contained unit. In all of the previous plans most of the children in each classroom have been approximately the same chronological age.[6] Diagram 4 shows an arrangement in which there are two ages in some of the classrooms. The children in the mixed-age rooms would generally remain there for two years.

After the five-year-old pupils have completed their first year, they are assigned to any one of three classrooms. In one of the rooms, most of the children would be six-year olds, but in the other two rooms there would be a mixture of six- and seven-year olds. On the right side of the diagram, two rooms are mixed-age classes and one is composed mostly of fourth-year students about the same chronological age.

In Diagram 4 most of the children in a mixed-age class remain there for two years. The younger half of the class remains a second year when it is then the older half of the class. It is not essential, however, that programs with mixed-age classes be conducted so that most pupils spend two years in a given room. The children could be moved each year. Diagram 5 illustrates this type of program.

By referring to Diagram 4, the reader can follow an individual as he progresses in reading during his four years in the primary unit. A child in classroom M who had completed level 7 at the end of his second year in the primary unit could continue in that room for another year and begin in the fall at level 9. At the end of that year he might be at level 10. For the next year — his fourth in the primary unit — he could be assigned to room Q where he might

---

[5]Diagram 4 is another example of Plan 2 of the three principal plans for implementing a nongraded program.

[6]An exception to this was the variation to Diagram 3.

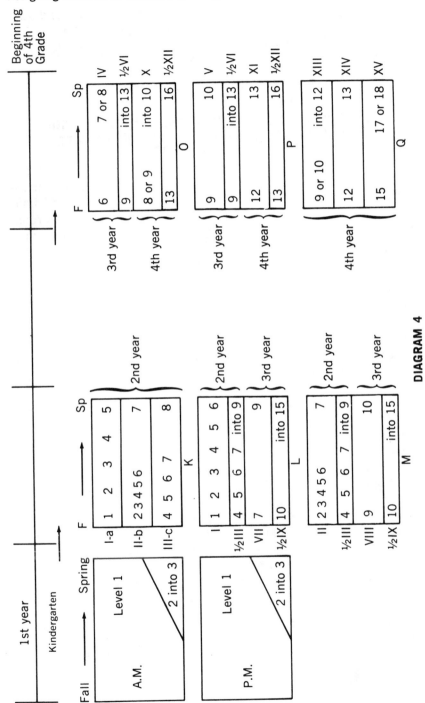

**DIAGRAM 4**

begin at level 12 and progress to 13. The following year he would move into 4th grade. The reader can experiment with other ways by which individual children might be assigned to classrooms as they move through the primary unit.[7]

The reading levels that are indicated for each classroom on this diagram are those for a particular aggregation of 50 to 60 children who enter kindergarten and progress through the primary unit. The exact reading levels that were offered in any given room would differ somewhat if a different aggregation of 50 to 60 children had been illustrated. This would be true for each new group of boys and girls who entered kindergarten and moved up through the primary unit. It is the pupils' reading levels that determine the instructional levels, not an arbitrary decision that certain levels will be studied in certain classrooms.

There are a few nongraded schools with mixed-age classes where three ages are placed together. In some of these schools, children spend three years in one room with the same teacher. Each year the oldest third of the class moves out and eight to ten beginners are added.

Partial inter-classroom achievement grouping is another feature of Diagram 4. The very slowest children of one age are not placed in a classroom with the most advanced children of the next age. By noting the reading levels in specific classrooms, the reader can observe this separation. Although the extremes have been separated, a wide range in reading levels still exists. A further reduction in the range in a given classroom could be effected, but this would represent an attempt at _full_ rather than _partial_ inter-classroom achievement grouping. Diagram 5 illustrates classroom assignments where there is full achievement grouping in reading.

Diagrams 2 and 4 are similar in that both involve partial achievement grouping. The only difference is the change from single to double-age classes. Since both diagrams show how the same aggregation of 50 to 60 children might progress in two different nongraded programs, the reader can follow a specific child as he moves from one classroom to another in Diagram 2, and then compare his progress in Diagram 4. In making the comparison, the reader

---

[7]In Diagram 4 most of the children who spend a year in classroom K would then progress to rooms O or P and be the younger pupils in these double-age rooms. After two years in these classes, most of the pupils would move to fourth grade. A few might need to spend an extra year in the primary unit however. Their room assignment is discussed later.

can note the age and reading levels of the other children who are in the same classes with this child. A table is provided in footnote 8 to facilitate the comparison of a child's progress through Diagrams 2 and 4.[8]

Educators who advocate the use of mixed-age classes in non-graded schools believe that there are certain advantages to this type of organization. One of the advantages frequently cited is the greater possibility of disguising the fact that a child spends an extra year in the primary program. As an example, let us follow an unusually slow reader, who, because of his reading and other reasons, needs to spend an extra year in the primary unit. He might begin in classroom K and by the end of the year progress to level 5. He could spend his next year in classroom O beginning at level 6 and perhaps progressing to level 7. In this room half of the pupils would be his own age and half would be a year older. This will

---

[8]Comparison of children's classroom assignments in Diagrams 2 and 4 — read across.

| DIAGRAM 2 | | DIAGRAM 4 |
|---|---|---|
| Children in room E | same as | Children in room K. |
| Children in room F | equally divided between | Rooms L and M. Roman numerals indicate exactly how the division was made. Roman numeral I in Diagram 4 corresponds to I in Diagram 2; ½ III in Diagram 4 represents one half of the children at III in Diagram 2. |
| Children in room H | equally divided between | Rooms L and M. Roman numerals indicate exactly how the division was made. |
| Children in room G | equally divided between | Rooms O and P. Roman numerals indicate exactly how the division was made. |
| Children in room I | equally divided between | Rooms O and P. Roman numerals indicate exactly how the division was made. |
| Children in room J | same as | Children in room Q. |

give him the experience of being in a room where there are boys and girls of different ages and where the situation is viewed as normal procedure.

The next year he might remain in classroom O and begin in the fall at level 8 or 9.[9] Some of the children will be his own age and others will be a year younger. At the end of this year, which would be his fourth in the primary unit, if he was not ready for fourth grade he would probably spend an extra year in the primary unit. He could be assigned either to classroom P where he might begin in the fall at level 12, or be placed in room Q. The placement of other children could be arranged so that a few his own age were in the room, but most of them would be at least a year younger. His age differential, however, would probably be somewhat less conspicuous than in a program with only single-age classes, since in mixed-age programs the pupils are more accustomed to being with others who are a different age.

The child described in the preceding paragraph could have been assigned to different classrooms than those indicated. Various alternative room assignments exist because in mixed-age classes an individual pupil's age difference is less of a distinguishing feature. For the same reason, the progress of children who take less than the usual number of years to progress through the primary unit may be less conspicuous. The reader can refer to the diagram to experiment with various ways by which such pupils could be assigned to classrooms.

In single-age rooms, the more able boys and girls are generally at the top of their class. Success comes easily and many leadership roles fall to them. In multi-age classrooms, these children might experience a year or two where leadership did not fall so quickly to them, for they could be assigned so that they were the younger children in a classroom of two age levels. Similar alternative placements exist for pupils who in a single-age classroom would normally be at the bottom of the class year after year.

There are other advantages claimed for mixed-age classrooms:

(1) At the beginning of the year, the older children are more familiar with instructional procedures than are the younger ones. Therefore, less teacher time is needed to start the class and teach appropriate classroom behavior, and there is more time to devote to the younger children who need the most help.

---

[9]He might instead be assigned to room P where he would remain for two years. Or after a year in room P he could move to room Q.

(2) The younger children, learning from their older associates, seem to develop more independent study habits and more self-reliance earlier than is the case in single-age classrooms.

(3) The older children gain social maturity from their experience of providing leadership for the younger boys and girls.

(4) Leadership qualities can sometimes be fostered in a shy child, because he can gain confidence by associating with some of the younger pupils in the room.

(5) Stereotyping of students can be reduced. For example, the tallest, shortest, fastest, slowest, or fattest does not necessarily remain in this position year after year. In his first year in the classroom, a child may be the smallest, but by the next year there may be younger "newcomers" who are smaller. The same is true in arithmetic or any other subject. The first year he may be working at a lower level relative to others in the class, but by the second year some of the newcomers would be at levels lower than he.

One of the concerns frequently expressed by teachers and administrators who are considering mixed-age classes is that the range of achievement levels would be wider than that found in single-age classes. If a comparison is made between the range of instruction required in mixed-age, nongraded classrooms and the single-level type of instruction actually provided in many single-age, graded schools, then of course there is a great difference. But when a comparison is made between the range of instruction required in mixed-age, nongraded classrooms and that required in single-age, nongraded classes, the difference is not nearly so great. The practice of nongrading has more effect on the range of instruction that is needed than does the change from single-age classes to those of two age levels.

If a teacher is already conducting a nongraded program in a single-age room, he is regularly providing instruction to children at different achievement levels. When pupils a year older are added, many of them would be working at achievement levels which the teacher was already offering. Only a few of the new children who were quite advanced would be ready for instruction at levels higher than that with which the teacher was already working. This would extend the range of instruction offered, but the increase would not be large next to the range already being provided. Once a teacher is providing multi-level instruction in a nongraded program, the addition of several higher levels might not seem as big a problem as it does to teachers and administrators who think primarily in terms of graded classrooms with single-level instruction.

If the plan for mixed-age classes also involves inter-classroom achievement grouping, the range in performance levels can be reduced in the subject used as the basis for grouping. In Diagram 4, which involves partial achievement grouping based on reading, the range in reading levels in some of the classrooms is not much greater than in the rooms of Diagram 1, which involves single-age classes. However, the performance spread in other skill subjects would not be similarly reduced. The range of reading levels could be further reduced if full achievement grouping was employed. Diagram 5 illustrates this situation.

In the content subjects, all of the pupils in a mixed-age class could study a given social studies or science topic at the same time. Elementary school children who have different abilities can work on the same topic provided instructional materials on different levels are used, and provided that the teacher is willing to accept various levels of understanding and performance.

In programs where boys and girls generally spend two years in a mixed-age room, it would be necessary to plan a sequence of topics so that repetition did not occur during the second year in the class. There would need to be a two-year cycle of topics; one sequence for the first year, and a different sequence for the next year. The following suggested program provides an example of the arrangement of topics in social studies. Classroom designations pertain to Diagram 4.

| | | |
|---|---|---|
| Classroom K | Each year: | Major units on school helpers, the fire department, and farm life |
| Classrooms L and M | One year: | Major units on school helpers, the fire department, and farm life |
| | Next year: | Major units on transportation, the post office, and the supermarket |
| Classrooms O and P | One year: | Major units on transportation, the post office, and the supermarket |
| | Next year: | Major units on shelter, clothing, and food |
| Classroom Q | Each year: | Major units on shelter, clothing and food |

By tracing the progress of individual children in Diagram 4, it can be noted that they would not repeat topics, provided the children passed through the primary unit in the usual four years. A child who spent an extra year in the primary unit, however, would repeat a set of topics somewhere along the line.

Teacher-cycling is often associated with mixed-age classes. If students spend two years in these classes, as illustrated in Diagram 4, teacher-cycling is a natural concommitant—the same teacher could work with the children for two years. Some educators believe that boys and girls benefit from a continued association with a teacher who knows them well. Teacher-cycling is not, however, a requirement with a mixed-age class, for a different teacher could be assigned to the room each year.

## Diagram 5

### A Nongraded School and Mixed-Age Classes with Full Inter-Classroom Achievement Grouping

This diagram illustrates a nongraded program that also includes arrangements for (1) mixed age classes, and (2) full inter-classroom achievement grouping.[10] Each class is a self-contained unit. Diagram 5 differs from Diagram 4 in two respects. One distinction is the greater degree to which achievement grouping has been introduced. The other difference is that in Diagram 5 the children would not generally spend two years in the same mixed-age classroom. At the end of each year, most of them would be reassigned.

It can be noted in Diagram 5 that the range of reading levels in each classroom has been reduced from what it was in Diagram 4.[11] It is also evident that in some of the mixed-age rooms there is an overlapping of reading levels for children who are two different ages. A teacher in one of the mixed-age rooms on the right side of the diagram might be able to combine the pupils of two ages for reading instruction, because the reading levels appear to be fairly similar. Actually, however, this might not be as feasible as it would seem. For instance, in room O some of the third-year students at level 9 in the fall (Roman numeral VII) may be ready for instruction that emphasizes certain aspects of reading that are different from those which need to be emphasized with fourth-year students at

---

[10]Diagram 5 is another example of Plan 2 of the three principal plans for implementing a nongraded program.

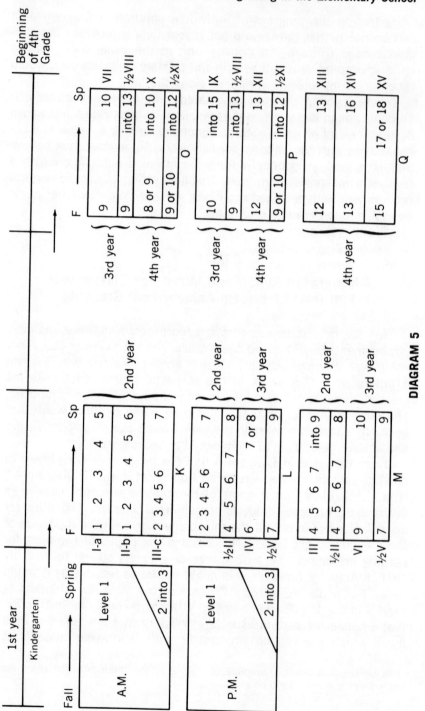

**DIAGRAM 5**

level 8 or 9. One reason for this might be that the children who are a year apart in chronological age are progressing at very different rates in reading.

Another factor, which should be considered when evaluating Diagram 5, is that although the children are closer together in their reading levels, this does not mean that there would be a corresponding reduction in the range of achievement levels in other subjects. This is one of the problems that attends a program of full achievement grouping. Other problems were mentioned in the discussion of Diagram 3. Diagrams 3 and 5 are similar in that both involve full achievement grouping. The only difference is the change from single-age to mixed-age classes. A table is provided in footnote 12 to facilitate the comparison of a child's room assignment in Diagrams 3 and 5.[12]

Although Diagram 5 involves mixed-age classes, the children would not generally spend two years in the same room. The reason for this stems from the effort that has been made to achieve full, inter-classroom achievement grouping in reading. By referring to Diagram 5, the reader will be able to observe that in most instances it would not be possible for a child who reached a given level in the spring of the year to remain in that room and begin work the following fall on the next level. He would have to be assigned to

---

[12] It is possible to compare the room assignments of individual children in Diagrams 4 and 5. The Roman numerals will facilitate the making of comparisons, but the conversion table below must be used. Read across:

| DIAGRAM 4 | | DIAGRAM 5 |
|:---:|:---:|:---:|
| I — a | same as | I — a |
| II — b | same as | III — c |
| III — c | same as | ½II and ½II |
| I | same as | II — b |
| ½III and ½III | same as | III |
| VII | same as | ½V and ½V |
| ½IX and ½IX | same as | IX |
| IV | same as | IV |
| ½VI and ½VI | same as | ½VIII and ½VIII |
| X | same as | X |
| ½XII and ½XII | same as | XIV |
| V | same as | VII |
| XI | same as | XII |
| XIII | same as | ½XI and ½XI |
| XIV | same as | XIII |
| XV | same as | XV |

another room. This would be necessary if the classes were to be kept as nearly homogeneous as possible in reading.

Diagram 5 can be used to trace an individual child as he progresses in reading during his four years in the primary unit. For instance, a child in Classroom L who had completed level 7 at the end of his second year in the primary unit could move to room M or O for his next year and begin in the fall at level 9. At the end of that year he might be at level 10. The following year, his fourth in the primary unit, he could move from room M to P, or from room O to P or Q. However he was assigned, he would begin at level 12. At the end of that year he could be assigned to fourth grade. The reader can experiment with the ways other children, including those who are especially bright or slow, might be assigned to classrooms as they move through the primary unit.

The curriculum in social studies and science would need to be planned so that a child would not repeat topics as he moved from one classroom to the next. One way to prevent repetition would

---

[12]Comparison of children's classroom assignments in Diagrams 3 and 5 — read across:

| DIAGRAM 3 | | DIAGRAM 5 |
|---|---|---|
| Children in room E | same as | Children in room K |
| Children in room F | equally divided between | Rooms L and M<br>Roman numerals indicate exactly how the division was made. Roman numeral I in Diagram 5 corresponds to I in Diagram 3; ½II in Diagram 5 represents one half of the children at II in Diagram 3. |
| Children in room G | equally divided between | Rooms L and M<br>Roman numerals indicate exactly how the division was made. |
| Children in room H | equally divided between | Rooms O and P<br>Roman numerals indicate exactly how the division was made. |
| Children in room I | equally divided between | Rooms O and P<br>Roman numerals indicate exactly how the division was made. |
| Children in room J | same as | Children in room Q |

be to offer sequences of topics in two-year cycles. For example, the social studies program might be planned as follows:

Classrooms K, L, M

> One year: Major units on school helpers, the fire department, and farm life
> Next year: Major units on transportation, the post office, and the supermarket

Classrooms O, P, Q

> One year: Major units on Indians, community, and food
> Next year: Major units on clothing, shelter, and communicating

By tracing the progress of individual pupils in Diagram 5, it can be noted that they would not repeat topics, provided that they passed through the primary unit in the usual four years. If a child needed an extra year, he might then have to repeat one year's sequence of topics.

## Team Teaching and Departmentalization

In the preceding sections of this chapter dealing with different ways to assign children to teachers in nongraded schools, each arrangement has involved a self-contained classroom. No mention has been made of either team teaching or departmentalization. Since these other practices usually involve the way children are assigned to teachers for instruction, and since they represent one of the principal ways by which a nongraded program can be implemented, it is appropriate to discuss them in this chapter.

The mere practice of team teaching or departmentalization does not guarantee that nongrading will occur. As proof of this, each can be found in certain graded schools. However, the program would be nongraded if the large aggregation of children involved in the team or departmentalized arrangement was regrouped from time to time during the day or week to form clusters or classes that work on different levels under the direction of different teachers. This method of working with children, it will be recalled, is one of the three principal ways to implement a nongraded program.

There is, of course, a difference between team teaching and departmentalization in elementary schools. If the former is to be practiced, it is necessary for all of the teachers in the team to work together in teaching each of the subjects for which the team approach is being employed. If, on the other hand, one teacher handles all of the instruction in one subject for two or three classes of children, and another conducts all of the instruction in a different subject for these children, this is known as departmentalization.

Instead of using additional diagrams to illustrate team teaching and departmentalized arrangements in nongraded programs, reference will be made to the five diagrams presented earlier in this chapter.

*Team Teaching.* Team teaching could be practiced in any one of the programs illustrated by the five diagrams. Several examples follow. Reference is made first to Diagram 1. It should be recalled that heterogeneous grouping was a feature of that Diagram. The two teachers for a pair of classrooms at any year in the primary program could enter into a cooperative teaching arrangement. For reading instruction, they might inter-mix the children in the two classes. During the reading period each day, one teacher might work with the slower third of the children from both classes. The other would meet with the rest of the pupils, many of whom would be more self-reliant and require less direct teacher supervision. The two classes might be housed in one, double-size room with movable partitions; or if regular rooms were used, the children could move back and forth between the rooms for reading.

Criteria other than general reading levels could also be used for re-arranging the classes. Pupils who needed more work in phonics might be assigned to one teacher for several weeks, while the other teacher worked with the remaining children. Some of the latter pupils might do individualized reading while the teacher worked with others to encourage a more creative interpretation of material they had read. The inter-mixing of pupils from two classes for reading might take place every day, or it might occur only on certain days. The frequency would depend on the wishes of the two teachers. There might be inter-mixing again for arithmetic instruction, and for work in other areas of the curriculum. Regrouping children in this fashion is similar in some respects to the Joplin Plan.

The staffs in certain schools have felt that team teaching can provide a way to help teachers conduct multi-level instruction. As indicated earlier in this book, it is a formidable task for teachers to conduct multi-level instruction, especially in a self-contained classroom where there is a full range of achievement levels in each of the subjects. In a team teaching arrangement children from two or more classes could be re-grouped from time to time during the day or week according to performance levels. Instruction in a given group could then be devoted to a narrower range of achievement levels. This type of team teaching arrangement might make it easier for teachers to offer a multi-level instructional program.

In the discussion of team teaching to this point, the program that has been described is a *thoroughly* nongraded one. Each teacher would attempt to provide multi-level instruction to the children assigned to him. If, on the other hand, he worked with the group assigned to him in a whole-group, lockstep manner, then of course the program would be only *partially* nongraded. But it would be at least partially nongraded because all of the children in the total aggregation would not be expected to do the same work.

In some schools, teaching teams comprise more than two teachers. Sometimes there are three or four members of a team plus a teaching assistant.

In Diagrams 2, 3, 4, and 5 where the boys and girls have been permanently assigned to classrooms on the basis of reading achievement, there might be less reason to inter-mix the children in a team teaching arrangement in reading. However, such arrangements could be developed in the other subjects. These arrangements would be similar to those discussed for Diagram 1. Each teacher might work with only part of the range of achievement levels in a given subject. (This again would be similar in some respects to the Joplin Plan.)

There might be times when all of the pupils in a team teaching arrangement could be brought together for work with one teacher. Viewing demonstrations or films, listening to stories or explanations, and participating in other assembly-type experiences are possible large-group activities. During this time the other teacher or teachers might be assisting or preparing for a later lesson. Some advocates of team teaching believe that twenty to twenty-five per cent of the time of elementary school children can be spent profitably in large-group activities involving 50 to 60 or more children. Other educators question whether it is desirable to spend this much time in large groups.

One aspect of team teaching might be particularly attractive to teachers in a thoroughly nongraded program. Confronted with the need to prepare materials and plan for instruction at more than one level in each of the skill subjects, teachers might want to consider ways to divide up this work. One may have a special interest in arithmetic and take the major responsibility for planning arithmetic instruction for two classes. The other would also contribute ideas for the arithmetic program, but he would rely on the first teacher to plan much of the work and prepare certain materials for this subject. Both teachers would actually work with the children in arithmetic, either by inter-mixing them or working with them in a self-contained arrangement.

The second teacher might have the major responsibility for planning the work and collecting materials for instruction in a different subject. Thus, each teacher would not have to do all of the preparatory work for each of the subjects. This might reduce, some-what, the burden felt by a teacher in a nongraded, *self-contained* classroom who must do everything himself to provide a program of multi-level instruction.

Team teaching can be practiced at both the primary and upper elementary levels. It has probably been tried more often, however, in the upper years of the elementary program. Whether it is really desirable or workable to conduct a program which involves the inter-mixing of children in team teaching arrangements in various subjects is viewed differently by various educators. Some believe that two, three, or four teachers in a team would find that it is not an easy task to work together to provide nongraded instruction for a large aggregation of, say, 55, 82, or 110 pupils. Careful plans for the regrouping and teaching of the children must be made for every part of the program that involves the team approach. For some teachers, the pressure of having to meet together time after time to make these arrangements for a large aggregation of students might become oppressive. The pressure would be somewhat less, however, if cooperative teaching was practiced in only one or two parts of the program. Goodlad and Anderson in their extensive writings suggest that nongrading in combination with team teaching offers the most desirable type of organization because it makes possible so many alternative ways to work with children.

*Departmentalization.* Diagram 1 can be used to illustrate one type of departmentalized, nongraded program. The two teachers for a pair of classrooms at any one year could conduct their teaching in a departmentalized manner. One could handle all of the work in reading while the other conducted all of the instruction in arith-metic. The first teacher would conduct reading for two periods. He might work with some of the children from both rooms for one period, while the other teacher worked with the remaining children in arithmetic. For the next period, the first teacher would work with the remaining pupils in reading, while the other conducted arithmetic with the boys and girls who had not studied it the first period. For the program to be thoroughly nongraded, each teacher would have to provide multi-level instruction for the children assigned to him each period.

Nongraded, departmentalized programs, where used at all, have usually been conducted in the upper years of elementary school programs. Achievement grouping and mixed-age classes have been important features of a number of these programs. One example of such a program follows. Let us assume that there are six teachers for the 180 children in the last three years of an elementary school. If the school was organized by self-contained classes, each teacher would have approximately thirty pupils. In a departmentalized arrangement, one teacher might teach arithmetic to all of the children. For the first period in the day, this teacher might work with the 36 children who are at the lowest levels of achievement. This class would probably span at least three years in chronological age. The next period, the teacher might work with 36 boys and girls whose range of achievement was a little higher than in the first class. Each of the other three classes during the day would be composed of pupils whose arithmetic achievement ranged a little higher than the previous class. With five classes a day of 40 to 45 minutes each, the teacher would have some time during the day to take care of his planning and paper work.

This program is a clear example of inter-classroom achievement grouping and mixed-age classes. Assigning children to a different arithmetic class each year would provide for the fact that as they grew older they would be able to do more advanced work. If an individual child made such rapid progress during the year that his placement would be decidedly more appropriate in a different class, he could be re-scheduled during the year. The arithmetic teacher could work with a particular class using the whole-class method of instruction, or he could provide multi-level instruction. If the latter, a thoroughly nongraded program would prevail in arithmetic—if the former, the program would be only *partially* nongraded, but it would be at least partially nongraded because some attempt was being made in the school's total arithmetic program to gear instruction to the needs of different groups of children.

If the work in reading, science, or any other subject was also departmentalized, assignment to classes could be made in each subject according to performance levels—thus, a child could be in a more advanced arithmetic class and a less advanced reading class. In a departmentalized plan, there is often the problem of assigning a specific child to the right class at the right time, because schedule conflicts are a troublesome aspect of the program. The plan works best, from a scheduling standpoint, in a large school where there are more teachers and classes, and therefore more alternate placements for a single child at any given period. Since most elementary schools are not sufficiently large, and since many educators still question whether children from ages nine to twelve should have so many different teachers, a modified departmentalized plan has been tried in some schools. The children work in several curriculum areas with one teacher for half of the day. Then for the other half of the day they are assigned to several different teachers for different subjects. The Dual Progress Plan is one illustration of such a program.

A full discussion of team teaching and departmentalization would require that many procedures and concerns not described here be included. A discussion of these other procedures and concerns has been omitted because they do not relate directly to nongrading. Only certain aspects of cooperative teaching and departmentalization which pertain to the operation of a nongraded program have been discussed.

## *Summary*

There are three principal plans for implementing a nongraded program—each involves a different way of assigning children to teachers. In the first of the three plans, placement is made in self-contained classes according to age. The children are heterogeneous in terms of academic performance. Diagram 1, which was one of several diagrams presented in this chapter, illustrates how children would move through this type of program.

In the second plan, placement in self-contained classes is on the basis of performance levels, and instruction is provided from one class to the next on different levels of difficulty. In this way interclassroom achievement grouping is practiced. Diagrams 2 and 3 illustrate different ways this plan might function when children in a given classroom are approximately the same age. Diagrams 4 and 5 show how the plan would work when there are pupils of mixed ages in a classroom.

In the third plan for implementing a nongraded program, a large aggregation of children is regrouped from time to time during the day or week to form clusters or classes that work on different levels under the direction of different teachers. This plan could be conducted as either a departmentalized program or one involving team teaching. An explanation was given of how team teaching arrangements could be introduced in Diagrams 1, 2, 3, 4, and 5. Nongraded, departmentalized programs were also explained briefly.

The five diagrams plus the examples of team teaching and departmentalization represent the principal ways nongraded programs have been conducted. That the principal ways are presented here together so that the reader has the opportunity to compare them, is an important feature of this book. A diagram of a graded program was also included for comparison purposes. Each diagram shows the same aggregation of 50 to 60 children starting at the kindergarten level and progressing year by year. Since the same group is used in each of the diagrams, the way a given child is assigned to classrooms in one diagram may be compared with his placement in the others.

No attempt was made in this chapter to suggest that a particular plan for nongrading represented the most desirable type of program. The staff members in a local school system should decide whether one of the programs described here, or some variation, would actually be workable or desirable in their system. Variations in the programs should certainly be considered, for the examples presented in this chapter are not meant to be exact blueprints. Their chief purpose is to provide a frame of reference and to stimulate thinking.

# 6

# A Report Form for Nongraded Schools

## Introduction

If a school staff is seriously interested in developing a nongraded program, modifications in many traditional practices will be needed. Some of these modifications have already been discussed. Another important change would be to alter the way in which pupils' work was evaluated and reported to parents.

In many of the schools where attempts have been made to develop nongraded programs, reporting practices have not been sufficiently revised. If teachers must continue to use a report card designed for use in a graded structure while they are urged to conduct their daily classroom work in a nongraded manner, both the children and the teachers will soon become confused and disillusioned. As a result, many teachers will question the wisdom of continuing the nongraded program, and its chances for success will have been seriously impaired.

In this chapter, an example of a report form for a nongraded school is presented. It appears on the next six pages. Although only one sample is shown, this is not meant to imply that it is the only one suitable for use in nongraded schools. It is provided solely for illustrative purposes—as something concrete to consider. If it stimulates thinking and leads to the consideration of other possible ways to report children's progress in a nongraded program, then it has served its purpose well.

There were two other reasons for including a specific example of a report form. First, few of the published materials on nongrading contain such a sample, and second, a survey by the writer indicated that in a number of schools that had attempted to develop nongraded programs, the reporting procedures were not consistent with the principles of nongrading.

The sample form presented here is limited to the primary years because this span of time is sufficient to illustrate the procedures which are involved. Reporting procedures for the upper elementary years could be developed in much the same way.

On the sample form, the method used to report a child's work in the skill subjects differs from that used to report his work in the content subjects. Because of this, the methods for each of these main areas of the curriculum are discussed separately.

# REPORT FORM — PRIMARY UNIT

Bard Elementary School                                    School year ( *1967/1968* )

( *Jack Smith* ) is in his ( *second* ) year of the continuous progress primary unit. This program begins with kindergarten and continues until the child enters fourth grade. Each child is helped to work at the level where he is and to make as much progress as possible. This report form has been especially designed for use in a continuous progress program.

Every child is marked in each subject three times a year. Instead of receiving a single mark in a subject, three are given. These are entered in the boxes at the top of each page.

The teacher will schedule a conference with each child's parents once a year in October. Other conferences may be arranged if desired.

---

# READING, ARITHMETIC, SPELLING, AND HANDWRITING

In these skill subjects, each child is encouraged to progress at his own rate through a series of tasks or levels. Different children in the same classroom will be working at different levels — some will do their work in greater depth than others.

Children who are progressing more slowly may need to spend extra time in the primary unit. Parents will be fully informed of such a need.

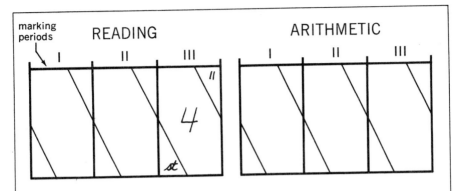

| MEANING OF THE THREE MARKS |

NUMBERS:     A NUMBER indicates the task or level on which your child is working.

| Reading Levels | Arithmetic Levels |
|---|---|
| 1 general readiness | 1 general readiness |
| 2 *Before We Read** | 2 cardinal idea of number: I |
| 3 *Sally, Dick and Jane* | 3 cardinal idea of number: II |
| 4 *Fun With Our Family* | 4 numeration system to 99 |
| 5 *Fun Wherever We Are* | 5 fundamental operations |
| 6 *Fun With Our Friends* | 6 measurement: I |
| 7 *More Fun With Our Friends* | 7 addition and subt. facts to 8 |
| 8 *The New We Three* | 8 problem solving: I |
| 9 *Friends Old and New* | 9 money |
| 10 *More Friends Old and New* | 10 problem solving: II |
| 11 *The New What Next* | 11 multiplication and div. facts to 12 |
| 12 *Roads to Follow* | 12 measurement: II |
| 13 *More Roads to Follow* | 13 preparation for carrying and borrowing |
| 14 *The New Tall Tales* | 14 $+ - \times \div$ to 18 |
| **Beginning of Fourth Grade** | 15 subt.: two figures with borrowing |
| 15 *Ventures: 1st half* | 16 beginning fractions |
| 16 *Ventures: 2nd half* | **Beginning of Fourth Grade** |
| 17 advanced reading | 17 div.: review of basic facts to 12 |
| 18 more advanced reading | 18 problem solving: III |
| | 19 rounding off large numbers |
| | 20 advanced arithmetic |

*The Scott Foresman Company series

LETTERS:     LETTERS indicate the effort your child is putting forth on a task. He is rated in terms of his <u>own</u> capabilities and background, not in terms of how he compares to other children.

st = Strong Effort
sa = Satisfactory Effort
l = Low Effort

SIGNS:     A SIGN indicates the degree of depth in your child's work as compared to that of other children who have performed the same task.

|| = Deals with material in a simpler manner.
•• = Deals with material in greater depth.
√ = Deals with material in an average manner.

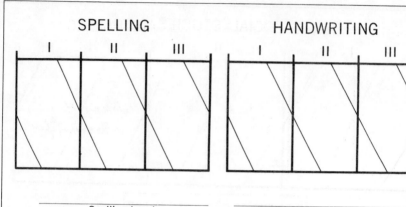

## SPELLING                                    HANDWRITING

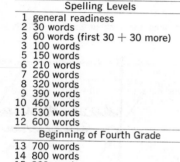

| Spelling Levels |
|---|
| 1  general readiness |
| 2  30 words |
| 3  60 words (first 30 + 30 more) |
| 3  100 words |
| 5  150 words |
| 6  210 words |
| 7  260 words |
| 8  320 words |
| 9  390 words |
| 10  460 words |
| 11  530 words |
| 12  600 words |

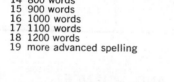

### Beginning of Fourth Grade

13  700 words
14  800 words
15  900 words
16  1000 words
17  1100 words
18  1200 words
19  more advanced spelling

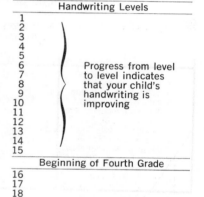

Handwriting Levels

1
2
3
4
5
6        Progress from level
7        to level indicates
8        that your child's
9        handwriting is
10       improving
11
12
13
14
15

### Beginning of Fourth Grade

16
17
18

Children are generally not introduced to the spelling program until they reach the _____
in reading.          (indicate level)

In handwriting, SIGNS indicate the
quality of your child's work at a
given level as compared to that of
other children who have worked
at that level.

||=Less legible
• •=Very legible
√=Average

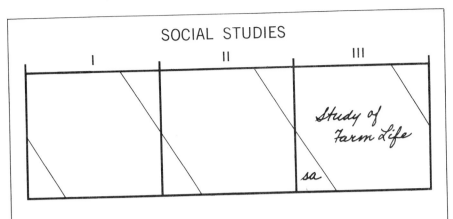

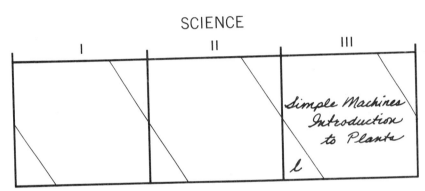

## SOCIAL STUDIES AND SCIENCE

In these content subjects all children in a classroom work together on the same topic at the same time. The topics studied during the last marking period are entered in the appropriate boxes. Some children are able to study a topic in greater depth, whereas other pupils deal with the topic in a simplified manner. "Depth of study" marks, and those for "effort," are entered at the sides of each box.

In social studies and science, children do not work ahead at varying rates through a series of levels as in the skill subjects.

Reporting procedures for:


Music

Art

Physical Education

General Behavior

Teacher's additional comments, if any. (Date each comment.)

_____

_____

_____

_____

_____

_____

_____


Request for parent-teacher conference, if desired.

_____

_____

_____

_____

_____

_____

_____

## Reporting Procedures in the Skill Subjects

The sample report form illustrates reporting procedures for the skill subjects which are different from those usually employed in traditional graded schools. To appreciate why the procedures are changed, it is necessary to recall some of the differences between graded and nongraded programs. An essential feature of the graded plan is that specific skills have been designated as the appropriate work for a given grade. All pupils in the grade are expected to learn these skills in a year's time. In keeping with the theory of graded school organization, instruction is not given either beyond or below that which is designated for the grade.

The skills which are designated as the appropriate work for a given grade are regarded as the standard for that grade. The standard plays an important role in evaluation procedures and reporting to parents, for each child in a grade is rated in terms of how well he measures up to it. Children who learn the designated skills easily are given A's or B's, whereas pupils who do not measure up to the standard are considered to be doing unsatisfactory work, and they are given D's or F's.

If instruction in the skill subjects is thoroughly nongraded, all of the children in a class are not expected to learn the same skills at the same time. Some pupils would learn more than others, and not all would have completed the same textbooks. Some children might advance to work which in a graded school would have been reserved for the next higher grade. They would study certain skills and topics in greater depth. Those who are making slower progress could do work that in a graded school would have been restricted to a lower grade, and they would study the basic skills and topics in a simpler manner. The teacher attempts to help each child begin at the level where he is and make as much progress as he can, in order to help him achieve success at his own level.

Since the skills work expected of children in a nongraded class differs from one child to the next, there is no uniform standard similar to that in a graded school against which to rate the way children perform. The type of marking system used in traditional graded schools would not be usable — new reporting procedures would be needed.

# Reporting Procedures in Reading

The sample report form conveys three kinds of information about a child's progress in reading: (1) the level at which the child is working, (2) the profoundness of his performance at this level, and (3) the effort he is putting forth. The following paragraphs contain a discussion of each of these dimensions.

In designing a report form for reading, it was necessary to have in mind a specific nongraded program. The one envisioned here for reading is divided into a series of levels, each involving the performance of various skills. When a child can perform these skills sufficiently well, it is considered that he has completed the level and is ready to begin working on the next level. Teacher judgment might be the sole criterion of whether he was ready for the next level, or standardized tests might also be used. In the case of the latter, the tests which accompany certain basal reading series provide one source of such measuring instruments.

On the sample report form, a child's first task in reading is to demonstrate that he can perform sufficiently well various general readiness skills. Two examples might be: (1) using language correctly in oral communication, and (2) detecting likenesses and differences visually. When a child is ready to work on pre-reading skills by means of more formalized procedures, he will have advanced to level 2. When he can demonstrate satisfactory performance of these skills, he will have advanced to level 3 which consists of the skills necessary to read the first pre-primer. He would progress in this manner through a series of levels.

Eighteen levels are shown on the sample report form. The last four consist of work that would have been reserved for the fourth and fifth grades in a graded program. In many nongraded schools, each level consists of one of the books in the basal reading series. The names of the books, instead of their grade designations, are often used to identify the levels, and this has been done on the sample report form. Specific reading skills could be listed instead, but many teachers and administrators have felt that such a list would require too much space on the report form, and would provide more detailed information than many parents would care to have. When too much information is given, sometimes there is difficulty in interpreting all of it.

There is another reason why a decision has been made in certain nongraded schools against listing specific skills — the sequence that is best for one child might not be best for another. If the sequence is printed on the card, a rigidity is imparted to the program which is undesirable in a nongraded school. Teachers might follow the sequence in its precise order, especially since parents would have questions if their child's progress deviated from the prescribed order. To explain why certain children were not following the standard sequence would be time-consuming for the teacher. By adhering too closely to a standard sequence of printed skills, one of the ways of providing for different abilities and patterns of learning would have been eliminated.

If the skills are not listed on the report form, this should not suggest that the faculty give little attention to them. Teachers should be informed which skills are the important ones to emphasize at each level. These could be indicated in the curriculum guide. The guide should also encourage teachers to modify the skills or change the sequence if this seems best in the case of an individual child.

Although the report form presented here identifies each reading level by the name of one of the books in the basal reading series, this does not need to limit a teacher to a program based entirely on a reading series. He might select only certain stories from the basal reader, but make considerable use of supplementary readers and/or trade books. The language experience approach or self-instructional workbooks might also be used. In a school where the language experience approach and individualized reading were the principal methods of instruction, the names of the basal readers could be omitted on the report form, and a sequence based on different activities substituted.

The eighteen reading levels indicated on the sample report form include several supplementary readers. These are levels 8, 11, and 14. Students who did not need this type of work could skip these levels.

Since parents will be interested to know how their child is progressing toward the goal of entrance to fourth grade, a fourth grade marker has been inserted in the sequence of reading levels on the sample report form. It has been assumed here that the nongraded program extends only to the end of the primary unit. If it continued upward through all of the elementary school years, a school staff might decide to show only a seventh grade marker on the report form.

At the end of each marking period the teacher would indicate on the report form the reading level at which the child was working. The teacher would also indicate the manner in which the child was performing his work. Two marks are used on the sample report form to provide this information: a mark to indicate the effort that a child has put forth, and a mark to indicate the degree of profoundness of his work at his own level.

Effort would be rated strong, satisfactory, or low. There would not be a uniform standard, but instead each pupil would be rated in terms of his own situation. Thus, a less capable child could receive a "strong effort" mark if *for him* he had worked hard. He would receive this mark even though his effort might appear less intense when compared to that expended by a child of greater resources.

When effort appeared to be low in reading, it would be necessary to weight various factors before entering a "low effort" mark on his report form. This mark should probably be assigned only when there is reason to expect that it is within the child's own power to exert more effort. If family circumstances, physical disabilities, or emotional problems are such that increased effort could not be expected until these conditions are ameliorated, then it would hardly help the child to receive a rating of "low effort." He should probably be marked "satisfactory effort," for in terms of his particular circumstances his effort may be all that could be expected. In such cases, the teacher could indicate on the report form that a conference is desired. The situation can then be discussed with the parents, and perhaps some means can be found to improve conditions.

The third mark for work in reading would indicate the profoundness of performance at a given level. The symbol "||" would mean that a child was working in a simpler manner on a task, whereas the symbol "··" would indicate that he was dealing with the material in considerable depth. Children who received the ·· symbol might have engaged in various enrichment activities and performed with more insight, or in a more imaginative manner.

In this dimension of the marking system a child's work at a given level would be evaluated against a standard for that level. The standard would consist of a range of performance extending from that which was less profound to that which was of greater depth. To help the teacher know what constitutes performance at the high or low end of the range, suitable explanations could be included in the curriculum guide for the level.

Although some educators might feel that a "depth of performance" mark was not necessary, parents sometimes want to know the manner in which their children are working at a given level. If this information is not provided by the school, parents may feel that the reporting system is inadequate, and urge a return to traditional procedures. This would be unfortunate in a school where an attempt was being made to conduct a nongraded program. It would seem that a reporting system should serve not only the purposes which the school feels are important, but also provide some of the information which parents desire.

Although the third mark showing depth of performance might appear on the surface to be similar to the traditional A — B — C — D — F marks in a graded school, it differs in certain ways. In a graded school all pupils in a given classroom are expected to work on the same skills. Some children are not ready to do this work, but are marked on how well they do it just the same. When they receive D's or F's, this indicates that their work is unsatisfactory, that they are not successful, and that they are failing and may have to repeat the work. All of this seems just a bit unfair since these children were expected to do work which they were not ready for in the first place.

In a nongraded school, the children in a classroom are not working on the same reading tasks. An individual would not begin a new level until the teacher felt he was ready, and would have reasonable success. As the child works at this level, recognition is given by recording the fact prominently on the report form. Each child will be making progress at his own level and the work will be paced so that he will not fail. As he proceeds, the teacher will also judge his depth of performance at the level where he is working. A low rating does not indicate that his work is unsatisfactory — it merely indicates that he does not perform on the level in as profound a way as the other children who have worked at that level.

Some of the children who received || marks would be those who worked in a simpler manner because of innate intelligence factors. Others receiving || marks might have the potential to deal with a subject in a more profound manner, but due to a deprived environment or physical disability they are not presently able to do this. Hopefully, a teacher, perhaps with the aid of other professional workers in the school, could give some indication to the parents of how these factors applied in the case of an individual child. Such information would be useful to parents as they try to help their children develop realistic goals for themselves.

An examination of the sample report form will reveal that of the three kinds of information provided regarding a child's reading work, the most prominent is the level at which he is working. This is given a central location, and the mark itself would be written larger than the other two marks entered at the sides. The reason for this is to emphasize the fact that regardless of his level, a child has been engaged in definite learning activities at school. It is important to the child that he gain recognition for the work he is doing. If he does not, there would seem to be good justification for his becoming discouraged. By looking back at previous reporting periods, both he and his parents can note his progress from one level to the next, no matter at what level he is working. The emphasis given to the fact that a child has been engaged in definite learning activities, regardless of his level of work, is quite different from the traditional reporting procedures in a graded school where marks of D or F imply to many parents that their child has done practically nothing.

The mark for depth of performance is given less emphasis. The reason for this is to place less importance on a rating which compares one child with another. Traditional report forms in graded schools have placed too great a stress on this one type of information. The purpose of a nongraded program is to help each child do the best he can at his own level and to be less concerned about how he compares with others.

## Reporting Procedures in Arithmetic and Spelling

The sample report form illustrates marking procedures in arithmetic and spelling which are similar to those in reading. The nongraded program, which these procedures are designed to accompany, is also quite similar to that used in reading. One small difference is that instead of having an entire textbook serve as one level, the book would be divided into several sections, each of which would be a level. From a child's standpoint this appears to be an advantage which provides for accomplishment in a shorter time.* There are twenty levels in the arithmetic sequence shown on the report form. The descriptive phrases which appear for each are the titles of different sections in a specific textbook series.

---

*Applying this same reasoning to the reading program, it would probably make sense to divide the primer into two or more sections, and to do likewise with several of the readers which follow.

Children in a given classroom would progress from one level to the next at varying rates. In addition to variations in rate, it would be possible to provide for other individual differences. Capable children might be expected to engage in various enrichment activities and demonstrate greater profoundness in their work at each level. If a teacher wished to report on individual differences not covered by the basic marks, he could write a note on the back of the form in the space for teacher comments. He might, for instance, comment about certain aspects of an individual's work which indicated initiative and self-reliance or imaginative thinking.

There are nineteen levels in the spelling sequence shown on the report form, each consisting of six lessons in a spelling textbook. Children might begin the spelling program after they had reached a certain level in reading. They would be allowed to advance at their own rate through the levels, and in some instances pupils would advance to lessons that would have been reserved for the next higher grade in a graded school. Some pupils might choose to do more than one lesson a week, whereas others of less ability might need to have a lesson broken into two parts so that they could study one part one week and the rest of the lesson the next week. In the latter case, it would take some children longer to complete a level, but this would be acceptable in a nongraded program. For a child to receive a "depth of performance" mark of ∙∙, he might be expected to have fewer spelling errors on the papers he wrote in connection with his work in other areas of the curriculum. He might also be expected to study certain words he had misspelled in his written work, and to do more with vocabulary development and word analysis techniques.

## Reporting Procedures in Handwriting

The sample report form illustrates marking procedures in handwriting which are similar to those in the other skill subjects. The nongraded program is also quite similar. There are eighteen levels consisting of sections from the workbooks in a basal series. A pupil could progress to a higher level when he could show that his handwriting had improved sufficiently for that level. Another whose handwriting was not nearly so well executed might also complete that same level provided the teacher felt his work showed definite improvement from when he began the level.

The standard of proficiency for a given level would be allowed to vary, because not all children in primary school will be able to write with a high degree of neatness even after considerable practice. If the standard was the same for all children it would take some of them several years to complete the first few levels. Such slow progress would be discouraging. The goal of the handwriting program in the primary unit is to help each child learn to write and then to improve his handwriting as much as possible with a reasonable amount of practice. Some children will become proficient with minimum practice, while others may devote considerable time to practice, and, although they improve, they may not be able to write very legibly.

On the report form would be entered the level on which a child was working, as well as a mark for effort and a mark indicating degree of legibility. If a child wrote very legibly, he would receive a mark of ∙∙, but if his handwriting was poorly formed by comparison to other children who had worked at that level, he would receive a mark of ||. A guide book showing samples of "average" handwriting for selected levels could be made available to teachers. The samples would provide a rough standard to use in judging the legibility of a particular child's handwriting. There could be one sample for use with the first 3 or 4 levels, a second sample for use with the next 5 or 6 levels, and a third for use with the last 7 or 8 levels.

If a particular child wrote especially well, he could be excused from further practice for a few months. At the end of that time he could complete several exercises at the next higher level in the workbook series to determine whether additional practice was needed. Each time he was excused from practice for a few months, a notation would be made in the teacher's record book that he had moved to the next higher level.

## Reporting Procedures in the Content Subjects

The sample report form displays marking procedures in social studies and science which are different from those in the skill subjects. These procedures are designed to accompany a specific nongraded program in social studies and science. In this program the work is not organized by levels through which children progress at varying rates. The tasks for children to accomplish consist of broad units of work rather than levels. Examples of primary units would be "The Fire Department" and "How Animals Prepare for Winter."

Everyone in a classroom would study a given unit at the same time. Although it might seem that this program of instruction differs little from that in a graded school, it will be recalled from an earlier chapter that the program can be quite different provided it is conducted in a *nongraded manner*. If the program was a graded one, the teacher would place great stress on having all children do work that was up to grade level standards. Pupils who did not meet this standard would be marked D or F, meaning that they had done unsatisfactory work. A single mark is usually the only indication of performance. Because of this, much attention is focused upon it, and undue importance attached to it.

If, on the other hand, instruction in the content subjects was conducted in a nongraded manner, it would be accepted by the teacher and explained to the children that pupils would vary considerably in the way they would engage in the study of a specific unit. For instance, as everyone in a classroom participates in a unit on The Fire Department, some would pursue their work with greater depth of insight. Others might deal with the material in a less complicated manner and grasp only the more obvious facts and concepts. It would not be expected that all children should perform according to one standard.

In a nongraded program the differing ways in which children perform are accepted. Each child is helped to do the best he can and to feel good about his accomplishment regardless of whether he is working in a simpler manner or in a more profound way.

Although it is entirely possible to conduct a whole class study of a broad unit in a nongraded manner, it is difficult to design a report form for such a program and avoid completely the weaknesses of the typical report card in graded schools. The reason for this stems from the fact that all children in a given class are working on the same unit. Since this is a whole-class project, the natural tendency to follow in rating performance is to compare it to some average expectancy for all children who engage in that project. In so doing, those of unequal background, maturation, and ability are rated against the same standard at the same time. This, of course, is exactly the problem with reporting practices in traditional graded schools. This problem, it seems, is an inevitable one when an important part of the social studies program consists of broad units in which all children participate at the same time.

There appear to be only several alternatives for dealing with this problem in a nongraded school:

(1) Omit from the report card any indication of the quality of work in the unit activities. One difficulty with this alternative is that many parents would be dissatisfied with a report which does not provide some indication of the manner in which the child is performing his work.

(2) Change the instructional program in the content subjects so that it is organized by levels similar to the work in the skill subjects. Then children could progress through the levels at their own rates and be evaluated against a standard for the level where they were working. In this plan not all pupils would be compared to the same standard at the same time. Reasons for not having a levels plan in the content subjects were indicated earlier.

(3) Include an evaluation of the quality of each child's work, but modify the practice so that it differs at least in a small way from the practice in typical graded programs. It is this third alternative that is used on the sample report form presented in this chapter.

Three types of information about a child's work in the content subjects are conveyed by the sample report form: the unit on which the class has been working, the effort the child is putting forth, and the profoundness of his work on the unit. As is indicated below, these procedures differ in a few small ways from reporting practices in graded schools.

(1) The name of the unit (or units) on which a child has worked during the reporting period is entered on the form. As viewed by the child, it is important to him that he has participated in the class project, and he wants due recognition for this. The report form gives recognition for such participation. Over a span of report periods, the accumulating entries of projects will indicate that a child has participated in a growing number of learning experiences. This is something in which he, and others concerned with his progress, can take pride.

In a typical graded program, the child might have participated in the same projects. But in the case of a child who receives a grade of D or F, the fact that he participated and that he did learn (albeit in his own manner) is not given proper emphasis.

If social studies and science activities are integrated in one broad unit, the teacher could enter the name of the unit in the social studies box on the report form, and the name of one or two related science topics in the science box.

(2) The effort put forth is recorded on the form. Since many students have the power to do something about their effort, there is an element of individual challenge here. And when a mark is given, pupils who have definitely tried will receive proper recognition.

(3) The mark used to denote quality of work indicates only that some children perform in a more profound manner than others. When a child receives a mark of ||, this does not mean that he has failed or that his work is unsatisfactory. It merely indicates that he has participated in the unit in a simpler manner than a number of the other children. This is accepted in a nongraded program.

(4) The "depth of study" mark on the sample report form is only one of three indications of a child's work in a content subject. Thus it is likely to be of less importance than if it was the single evaluation to appear on the report. Also, the mark is not given a central place on the form, and this contributes to its de-emphasis. The main entry is the listing of the unit or units on which the child has worked. Hopefully, the use of three entries would suggest that there is more than one kind of information that is important.

As already indicated, there are problems in using a "depth of study" mark in connection with a nongraded program in the content subjects where the entire class engages in the same unit study. These problems become more troublesome in the case of mixed-age classes and in schools where pupils have been assigned to classes according to performance levels.* In both of these situations there is the question of what standards would be used for evaluating children's work. Would the standard for the younger ones in a double-age class differ from that for those who are older? In schools where inter-classroom achievement grouping is practiced, would the same standard be used for pupils in the lower achieving class as was used for those in the higher achieving class? The response would seem to be affirmative in both cases, but this would yield a reporting system that was not completely consistent with the principles of nongrading. It appears that the principles must be compromised somewhat when a "depth of performance" mark is used in a program where all children study the same unit topic at the same time.

In the space for comments on the report form, a teacher would be able to indicate special work a child had done in the content

---

*Diagrams 2, 3, 4, and 5 in Chapter Five illustrate these situations.

areas. Certain children, working as individuals or in small groups, might have been encouraged to investigate topics of special interest to them. Hopefully, a teacher would encourage activities of this type, for this is another way to provide for individual differences.

The sample report form does not include a section devoted to the various work-study skills useful in studying the content subjects. Although children would surely be introduced to some of these skills in the primary years, concentrated work would probably come when they were older. The report form for the upper elementary years could show progress in learning these skills. The work could be organized by levels through which the children might proceed at varying rates.

## Other Reporting Procedures

Reporting procedures for music, art, physical education, and general behavior are not discussed here, but ways to evaluate children's performance in these areas would certainly need to be developed. As indicated previously, the report form would also include space for the teacher to make brief comments regarding special work a child had done. This space should be sufficiently large so that a teacher could present information he felt was important. He might, for instance, wish to comment about the stories a child was writing or the independent study activities he was pursuing. If a child was engaged in pupil-team instruction for some aspect of his work, the teacher might wish to discuss this. The teacher would also enter a note here if an extra year in the primary unit was necessary. As soon as a school staff felt this possibility existed, the parents should be notified. If the staff felt such information could be conveyed better in a conference, the teacher could use space on the back of the report form to make a written request for such a conference.

The report form described here would be sent home three times a year. More frequent reporting periods are not necessary because children do not change that rapidly. Also, if reports are sent more often, this means that teachers must devote more time to reporting procedures, and that less time is available for planning instruction. Teachers need all the time they can get if they are to plan the varied kinds of instruction necessary in a nongraded program.

Teachers would use a fresh report booklet for each year a child spends in the primary unit, since there is only space on the form for one year's marks. The form itself, however, is the same for all of the years after kindergarten and before fourth grade. A different form would be needed for the kindergarten year, which is the child's first year in the primary unit. A child's report booklet would be sent with him when he was assigned to another teacher, so that the teacher would know the approximate levels where he is working.

An added dimension of home-school communication might be a parent-teacher conference with each family in the fall of the year, with additional conferences being held if either a teacher or parent requested them. The fall conference would provide teachers and parents with an opportunity to become acquainted and would make it possible for the teacher to learn more about a child's life outside of school. The latter information would be helpful to the teacher as he plans his instructional program so that children of different backgrounds can make progress at their own levels. Released time should be provided for conducting some of these conferences — it is expecting too much of teachers if they are to hold all of the conferences after school hours. Teachers already have more than enough to do to plan and coordinate a multi-level instructional program in a nongraded school.

Some educators believe that report forms should not be used, and that instead, the reporting procedures should consist entirely of conferences and/or progress letters. These other procedures, it is suggested, provide more flexibility than a report card; therefore they should be used in a nongraded program, since one of the main reasons for having such a program is to provide more flexible ways of dealing with individual children.

There is no doubt that conferences and progress letters provide more flexibility in reporting pupil progress. Individual differences can be explained and each report can be tailored to a specific child, but this flexibility is also a potential hazard. Teachers may be too general in their comments, in which case many parents will feel dissatisfied. Teachers may also differ widely in the way they interpret evaluative criteria to parents. This would be confusing to parents and cause many to wish for a reporting system with a more clearly defined structure.

It is possible that in the case of some teachers and administrators the special appeal of conferences and progress letters is that their flexible nature makes it possible to get by without a clearly defined structure. Certain school staffs may have been unable to agree on specific criteria for evaluating children's work, and as a way around this dilemma conferences or progress letters were adopted. Each teacher could then follow his own system. Many educators would question such a reporting program, because of the many chances for inconsistencies which would cause parents, children, and teachers to become confused.

If a school staff is able to develop specific evaluative criteria, there are arguments in favor of presenting this information on a report form, rather than rely solely on conferences or progress letters. Many teachers, and parents too, prefer a reporting program with a clearly defined structure. It provides something in common for both parties to consider. The structure is more apt to be clear when it appears in printed form than when a different oral or written explanation is made to each of four or five hundred parents in an elementary school. There is also an element of continuity from one year to the next even though a child moves from one teacher to another. The latter is an especially important consideration in schools where there is a high rate of staff turnover.

When a report form is used to convey basic information about a child's work in school, parent-teacher conferences can be devoted to other important functions. These might include answering questions or trying to clarify misunderstandings, showing samples of a child's work, learning from parents more about a child's out-of-school life, and making plans for his future work and play activities. The conference also provides a good opportunity to help parents gain insights about their child's potential in various areas. Parents need to be helped to consider this important factor so that the expectations they have for their children can be reasonable.

## Summary

In this chapter a report form for a nongraded primary school has been described. A nongraded program requires reporting procedures which are different from the traditional report card in graded schools. The traditional card has generally presented only one kind of information, namely, a rating which shows how a child's work compares to the standard for his grade. The sample report form presented in this chapter provides three types of information for each subject: (1) the particular task on which an individual child is working — his task may differ from that of the next child, (2) his effort on this task, and (3) the degree of profoundness in his performance of the task. It was suggested that marks in these three areas would provide a better representation of a child's performance than the single mark found on traditional report cards.

Although an exact plan for a report form was presented in this chapter, this has been done for illustrative purposes only, and is not meant to imply that it is the single, most desirable plan. Other suitable procedures could surely be devised. A specific plan was included because it is the writer's belief that many teachers and administrators want clear examples of how new ideas might be put into practice. After studying a specific, illustrative plan, it is often easier to understand the new ideas and to think about alternative procedures.

There is always danger in being specific about something, for there are more opportunities to criticize an idea that is explained in detail than if only a general statement of it is presented. Since specific examples were set forth in this chapter, and elsewhere in the book, it is only natural that they will evoke questions and disagreements. This, however, is as it should be, for the illustrations are not meant to be final solutions. Instead, they serve as points of reference which hopefully will stimulate thinking and lead to the consideration of other possible procedures.

# Selected Bibliography with Annotations*

**Section One** of this bibliography contains materials which deal with the general topic *the nongraded school*. **Section Two** includes materials which describe various educational practices that could contribute to the implementation of nongrading. The reader's attention is called especially to Section Two, because the publications there deal with a dimension of nongrading which is not treated adequately in many of the materials appearing in Section One.

Most of the references cited in this bibliography are recent. For a comprehensive list of earlier materials, readers should refer to the bibliography in the book by John I. Goodlad and Robert H. Anderson, *The Nongraded Elementary School*, published in 1963.

## I. The Nongraded School

Ball, Lester, "The Elementary School of 1980," *The Elementary School Journal*, LXV (October, 1964), 8-17.
   Ball suggests that the educational program include nongrading and team teaching.
Beggs, David W. and Edward G. Buffie, (eds.), *Nongraded Schools in Action*. Bloomington, Indiana: Indiana University Press, a forthcoming book — 1966.

---

*A distinction is made between chapters in a cited book, and those in this book: for example, cited book: chapter one; this text, Chapter One.

This volume presents a selection of articles by twenty-five educators and practitioners who discuss the concept of nongraded schools from various viewpoints and provide case histories of a number of nongraded elementary and high school programs. The articles were especially prepared for this volume.

Brown, B. Frank, *The Appropriate Placement School: A Sophisticated Nongraded Curriculum.* West Nyack, New York: Parker Publishing Company, Inc., 1965.

The ideas for nongrading presented in Brown's book are similar to those in his earlier volume (see next entry in this bibliography). In the earlier volume, he describes only the nongraded high school, whereas in the more recent book he has included a brief discussion of nongrading at the primary, intermediate, and junior high levels (chapters four, five, and six). The plan he advocates for the intermediate school and junior high school is the same as his plan for the senior years: namely, that there be mixed-age, departmentalized classes organized according to achievement levels. A program of this type is described in Chapter Five, this text, in the section entitled "Departmentalization."

In the primary school, the program would not be departmentalized; children would be assigned to self-contained, mixed-age classrooms and there would be full inter-classroom achievement grouping based on reading. Unfortunately, Brown's explanation of the primary program is rather sketchy. He does not discuss how instruction in the various school subjects would be conducted nor exactly how children would move through the program. The plan appears, however, to be similar in many respects to Diagram 5 in Chapter Five of this text.

Brown emphasizes time and again in his book that there needs to be more variation in content for children of different ability. This is a very important dimension of nongrading in his opinion. He also stresses that the curriculum for children of all levels should be less rigidly geared to basal textbooks, and instead involve more emergent learning experiences stemming from a variety of instructional materials and procedures.

\_\_\_\_\_, *The Nongraded High School.* Englewood Cliffs, New Jersey: Prentice-Hall, Inc., 1963.

Brown describes the nongraded program he helped to develop at Melbourne High School, Melbourne, Florida. In each of the major subject areas, a series of classes is offered extending from those which are at a remedial level to those which are at an advanced level equivalent to college work. Since each class functions at a different level, the program is illustrative of one type of levels plan. For a given subject, a child is assigned to the class which is the appropriate one in terms of his level of achievement. Standardized tests are used to determine achievement levels in each subject.

In a given mathematics class there may be first-year high school students as well as those in their second or third year. These children are all working at about the same level in mathematics. These are mixed-age classes. There is no such thing as "sophomore" English or "freshman" Math. A child may be in a more advanced Mathematics class but attend a less advanced English course.

In Chapter One of this text, it is stated that there are three principal ways to implement a nongraded program. Melbourne High School is illustrative of the third way: the program is departmentalized and children are assigned to teachers according to performance levels. This is a clear example of achievement grouping. An attempt is made to reduce the range of performance levels with which a given teacher must work.

Brown's program would be easy to establish in a large, departmentalized school, because the multiplicity of classes would make it possible to schedule an individual child into classes which were the *right* ones for him. The program would be more difficult to implement in elementary schools because these are usually neither large nor departmentalized. Several of the examples in Chapter Five of this text, in the section entitled "Team Teaching and Departmentalization," illustrate, at the elementary level, some of the practices Brown has described.

In Brown's book, chapters one, two, and nine are particularly interesting.

Carbone, Robert F., "A Comparison of Graded and Nongraded Elementary Schools," *The Elementary School Journal,* LXII (November, 1961), 82-88.

Carbone's research is mentioned frequently in the literature because his findings are not supportive of the nongraded school. A review of his work reveals that in selecting graded and nongraded schools for inclusion in the study, sufficient attention was not given to differences in teaching practices in the two types of schools. For this reason, little significance can be attached to the findings. Carbone apparently became aware of this problem, for in evaluating his work he says that if a program is to be thoroughly nongraded, instructional practices must be altered and teachers must have the materials necessary to individualize the program.

Dean, Stuart E., "Nongraded Schools," Education Briefs No. 1, OE-20009. Washington, D.C.: Office of Education, 1964.

    This twenty-nine page pamphlet provides an informative introduction to nongrading. It contains a bibliography.

DiLorenzo, L. T. and R. Salter, "Cooperative Research on the Nongraded Primary," *The Elementary School Journal,* LXV (February, 1965), 269-77.

    The authors point out that in a number of "so called" nongraded schools nothing has really been changed except to remove grade labels and use different terms in talking about the program. There have been few changes in teaching practices, in what happens to the child, or in what is expected of him.

    Various research studies that pertain to nongrading are cited in the bibliography.

Dipasquale, Vincent C., "Dropouts and the Graded School," *Phi Delta Kappan,* XLVI (November, 1964), 129-33.

    This is a clearly written presentation of various features of graded and nongraded schools.

Dufay, Frank R., *Ungrading the Elementary School.* West Nyack, New York: Parker Publishing Company, Inc., 1966.

    Dufay describes the nongraded program which he and his staff developed in the elementary school where he is principal — Parkway School, Plainview, Long Island. The program is similar to the one illustrated in Diagram 3, Chapter Five, this text, if the variation to Diagram 3 (mentioned at the end of the description) is considered. Dufay explains in detail the procedures for assigning children to teachers in the nongraded plan at Parkway School.

    There are several differences between Dufay's book and this one: (1) He has described what happened in one school, whereas this text presents the differing procedures in various schools. (2) He has devoted considerable space to how he proceeded step by step to introduce the program to the teachers and parents. Although this aspect of the subject is not discussed here, more is said about instructional procedures in a nongraded program. (3) In addition, this text deals with the pros and cons of various practices in nongraded schools.

Goodlad, John I., (ed.), *The Changing American School,* Sixty-fifth

Yearbook of the National Society for the Study of Education, Part II. Chicago: University of Chicago Press, 1966.

Chapter five entitled "School Organization: Nongrading, Dual Progress, and Team Teaching" is relevant.

_____, "Inadequacy of Graded Organization, What Then?" *Childhood Education,* XXXIX (February, 1963), 274-77.

_____, "Meeting Children Where They Are: Nongraded Schools," *Saturday Review,* XLVIII (March 20, 1965), 57-59ff.

This is one of Goodlad's most interesting articles. He discusses certain aspects of the nongraded, team teaching program at the University Elementary School, University of California, Los Angeles.

_____, "Toward Improved School Organization," in *Elementary School Organization,* yearbook issue of *The National Elementary Principal,* XLI (December, 1961), 60-127.

Among other things, Goodlad discusses some of the problems of using regular, standardized, achievement tests in research designed to compare graded and nongraded programs.

_____, and Robert H. Anderson, *The Nongraded Elementary School,* rev. ed. New York: Harcourt, Brace & World, Inc., 1963.

This is a particularly valuable reference for those interested in nongrading. (For additional comments, see Chapter Two, this text, section entitled "Contributions of Goodlad and Anderson.")

Haas, Arthur, "First-Year Organization of Elmcrest Elementary School: a Nongraded Team Teaching School." *American School Board Journal,* CLI (October, 1965), 22.

Halliwell, Joseph W., "A Comparison of Pupil Achievement in Graded and Nongraded Primary Classrooms," *The Journal of Experimental Education,* XXXII (fall, 1963), 59-64.

Halliwell summarizes other research studies and presents findings from his own project. He discusses some of the problems involved in conducting research in this area.

Hillson, Maurie, (ed), *Change and Innovation in Elementary School Organization: Selected Readings.* New York: Holt, Rinehart and Winston, 1965.

Part six deals with nongrading. The sections of the book which deal with ability grouping, team teaching, and departmentalization are also relevant.

Inlow, Gail M., *The Emergent in Curriculum.* New York: John Wiley & Sons, Inc., 1966.

Among other things, Inlow discusses the advantages and

shortcomings — real or alleged — of nongrading (pp. 316-20).
He also discusses the possible limitations of team teaching
(pp. 300-302).

Johnson, Glenn R., "Lots of Smoke, But Little Fire," *The Educational
Forum*, XXIX (January, 1965), 159-64.

McDaniel, W. P., "Lemasters Elementary School Changes to a
Workable Nongraded System," *School and Community*, LI (May,
1965), 14-15.

McDaniel describes a nongraded program which involves
mixed-age classes and inter-classroom achievement grouping.
The program has some of the features of the Joplin Plan.

Morgenstern, Anne, (ed.), *Grouping in the Elementary School*. New
York: Pitman Publishing Corporation, 1966.

This collection of readings explores three organizational patterns for grouping children for instruction in the elementary
school: ability grouping, team teaching, and nongraded grouping.
The section on nongrading includes two reprints of articles:
one by Robert H. Anderson and John I. Goodlad, and the other
by Madeline Hunter.

The selections which deal with ability grouping and team
teaching are perhaps more helpful than those on nongrading. Of
particular interest is the report of a study by Miriam Goldberg
and A. Harry Passow entitled "The Effects of Ability Grouping."

NEA Research Division, "Nongraded Schools." Washington, D. C.:
NEA Research Division, May, 1965.

This twenty-page pamphlet presents an interesting overview
of nongrading. There is information about history and trends,
how it works, grouping, research efforts, and programs in representative schools. There is also a bibliography.

Sloan, Fred, A. Jr., "A Nongraded Social Studies Program for
Grades Four, Five, and Six," *The National Elementary Principal*,
XLV (January, 1966), 25-29.


## II. Educational Practices That Could Contribute
## to the Implementation of Nongrading

*Audiovisual Instruction*, VIII (October, 1963).

This issue contains several articles (pp. 570, 574, and 583)
which deal with the use of filmstrips and tape recorders for
independent learning in elementary school classrooms. Photo-
graphs show children using these devices.

Austin, Mary C. and Coleman Morrison, *The First R: The Harvard Report on Reading in the Elementary Schools*. New York: The Macmillan Company, 1963.

In chapter three the authors discuss nongraded programs and ways to provide for children's individual differences.

Bair, Medill and Richard G. Woodward, *Team Teaching in Action*. Boston: Houghton Mifflin Company, 1964.

Chapter eight is especially interesting. It explains the daily programs for two elementary school children in a nongraded, team teaching program. The situation described is one that involves a large team of teachers and extensive cooperative arrangements.

Beggs, David W. and Edward G. Buffie, (eds.), *Independent Study*. Bloomington, Indiana: Indiana University Press, 1965.

Various independent study practices which elementary school teachers have found to be workable are described in chapter five. This topic is relevant because the nature of nongraded programs almost requires that children do more of their learning by engaging in various forms of independent study.

Black, Hillel, "A School Where Children Teach Themselves," *Saturday Evening Post*, CCXXXVIII (June 19, 1965), 80-85.

This is an account of a suburban St. Louis elementary school where a nongraded, team teaching program was developed. John I. Goodlad served as a consultant. One of the most interesting features of the school is the emphasis on independent study. As individual children progress beyond their beginning work in the basic skills, they spend an increasing amount of time in various forms of independent study — up to one-half of the school day for older students. The building was constructed with a large learning materials center in a location central to the other instructional areas. Rather than having regular size classrooms, the building is divided into various instructional areas with different types of movable partitions.

Cawelti, Donald G., "Creative Evaluation Through Parent Conferences," *The Elementary School Journal*, LXVI (March, 1966), 293-97.

Cawelti suggests techniques teachers could use to help parents discuss some of the non-academic factors in their child's life. Information about such factors might be helpful to teachers working in a nongraded program where an attempt is made to provide for children's individual differences.

Cleland, Donald T. and Elaine C. Vilscek, (eds.), _Individualizing Instruction in Reading_, Conference on Reading. Pittsburgh: University of Pittsburgh, 1964.

A report by Vilscek entitled "Self-directive and Corrective Materials" contains a list of various self-directive and self-correcting teaching materials in reading which are available commercially. Other interesting reports are: "The Pittsburgh Experiment in Team Teaching," "A Concept of Personalized Reading" (individualized reading), "Augmenting the Basal Reader," and "Grouping to Provide for Individual Differences."

Daniel, Mary Ann, "You Can Individualize Your Reading Program Too," _Elementary English_, XXXIII (November, 1956), 444-46.

Darrow, Helen Fisher and R. Van Allen, _Independent Activities for Creative Learning_. New York: Bureau of Publications, Teachers College, Columbia University, 1961.

Darrow and Allen describe fifty-one independent work activities which are pupil initiated and which encourage the use of a child's own ideas to create and interpret. These activities differ from those in which pupils are told exactly how to proceed step by step, such as with certain commercial materials for self-instruction.

Draper, Marcella K. and Louise H. Schwietert, _A Practical Guide to Individualized Reading_, rev. by May Lazar, Bureau of Educational Research, Publication 40. New York: Board of Education, 1960.

Of the various books on individualized reading, this is one of the most helpful.

Durrell, Donald D. and others, "Adapting Instruction to the Learning Needs of Children in the Intermediate Grades," _Journal of Education_, CXLII (December, 1959), 1-78.

In the search conducted by the author of this text for information concerning the ways teachers work with children in nongraded programs, Durrell's presentation was one of the most interesting that was found. It is a report of a pilot program in several elementary schools. Durrell and his associates describe the way children were helped to pursue their work in the major curriculum areas by means of sub-group, pupil-team, and individualized instruction.

Egerton, Alice K. and Ruth W. Twombly, "A Programed Course in Spelling," _The Elementary School Journal_, LXII (April, 1962), 380-86.

Local teachers prepared a programed course in spelling which third grade children used for self-directed study. The students worked independently and at their own rates with the materials. Tests for each lesson were administered by a tape recorder which pupils operated.

Eisman, Edward, "Individualized Spelling," *Elementary English*, XXXIX (May, 1962), 478-80.

Eisman relates how spelling instruction was individualized in a third grade class.

Flournoy, F., "Meeting Individual Differences in Arithmetic," *Arithmetic Teacher*, VII (February, 1960), 80-86.

Flournoy lists, but does not describe in detail, the teaching and organization practices which can be used to provide for children's individual differences in arithmetic.

Henry, Nelson B., (ed.), *Individualized Instruction*, Sixty-first Yearbook of the National Society for the Study of Education, Part I. Chicago: The University of Chicago Press, 1962.

The authors who contributed to this yearbook deal mainly with the nature of children's individual differences and the need to provide for them. Less attention is given to the details of how teachers in elementary schools might actually conduct programs which provide for these differences.

Johnson, Alta, "Arithmetic Individualized," *Mathematics Forum*, published by Scott Foresman and Company, Chicago, VII (Spring, 1965), pp. 1 ff.

Johnson tells how she helped the children in her class use a standard arithmetic text in such a way that they could progress at their own rates.

Kierstead, Reginald, "A Comparison and Evaluation of Two Methods of Organization for the Teaching of Reading," *The Journal of Educational Research*, LVI (February, 1963), 317-21.

Kierstead describes a program in which the Joplin Plan was used as a way to ungrade the reading program.

Moench, L., "Individualized Practice in Arithmetic: A Pilot Study," *Arithmetic Teacher*, IX (October, 1962), 321-29.

Moench explains how children in an elementary school classroom worked at different levels in arithmetic by means of regular textbooks which had been cut into booklets. The booklets covered a range of several grades.

Otto, Henry J. and others, *Four Methods of Reporting to Parents*. Austin, Texas: The University of Texas, 1957.

Otto and his associates studied four reporting systems including grade cards, progress letters, and parent-teacher conferences. Parents, teachers, and pupils were asked many questions about their reaction to these reporting methods. The findings are summarized by Otto and are quite interesting. He found that the parent-teacher conference was the preferred method.

Parker, Don H., *Schooling for Individual Excellence*. New York: Thomas Nelson & Sons, 1963.

Chapters sixteen through twenty deal with the problems of providing instruction suitable for children who differ widely in performance levels.

Parker, Don H. and Genevieve Scannell, *Individualized Learning Through the Reading Laboratory Series*. Chicago: Science Research Associates, Inc., 1963.

The need for multi-level instruction in reading and the way in which the SRA materials for self-instruction meet this need are explained in this booklet.

Petty, Mary C., *Intra-class Grouping in the Elementary School*. Austin, Texas: University of Texas, 1953.

In chapter nine Petty describes the ways teachers in this study conducted sub-group instruction in reading and arithmetic. Chapter ten deals with the materials the teachers used.

Robinson, Helen, (ed.), *Reading Instruction in Various Patterns of Grouping*. Chicago: The University of Chicago Press, 1959.

The articles by John I. Goodlad (pp. 20-25) and by John M. Bahner (pp. 95-98) deal with nongraded, team teaching programs for reading instruction at the primary and intermediate levels.

Strang, Ruth, "Effective Use of Classroom Organization in Meeting Individual Differences," in *Meeting Individual Differences in Reading*, (ed.) H. Alan Robinson. Chicago: The University of Chicago Press, 1964, pp. 164-70.

Thomas, R. Murray and Shirley M. Thomas, *Individual Differences in the Classroom*. New York: David McKay Company, Inc., 1965.

These authors discuss the intellectual, artistic, and physical differences of children and some of the ways teachers and schools provide for these differences.

Veatch, Jeannette, *Reading in the Elementary School*. New York: The Ronald Press Company, 1966.

In chapter one, Veatch outlines a nongraded reading program involving the *language experience approach* for beginning reading and *individualized reading* for children who have progressed beyond the initial stages of instruction. She explains this program in detail in subsequent chapters. Chapter five contains an excellent discussion of independent work activities. Chapter seven presents ideas about sub-group instruction in a program of individualized reading.

Washburne, Carleton W., "Adjusting the Program to the Child," *Educational Leadership*, XI (December, 1953), 138-47.

In his interesting, clear style of writing, Washburne explains the need to provide for children's differences. He draws upon his many years of experience in elementary education to suggest ways to do this.

Wolfson, Bernice J., "Individualizing Instruction," *NEA Journal*, LV (November 1966), 31-33.

Wolfson states that the most suitable content and best sequence of learnings for one child are not necessarily the most desirable for another student. For an instructional program to be thoroughly individualized, provision for variations in content and sequence are just as important as provision for variations in rate of learning. There should be considerable opportunity for individual pupils to select areas of study which are of particular concern to them.

Yoakam, G. A., (ed.), *Providing for the Individual Reading Needs of Children*, Conference on Reading. Pittsburgh: University of Pittsburgh, 1953.

The following reports are especially interesting: "Providing for Individual Differences Through Differentiated Material," "How to Teach a Class Grouped for Differentiation in Basal Reading," "Problems Involved in Differentiating Materials to Provide for the Individual Reading Needs of Children," "Problems Involved in Providing for the Individual Needs of Children."

## III. Other References

Hansen, Carl F., *The Four-track Curriculum in Today's High School*. Englewood Cliffs, New Jersey: Prentice-Hall, Inc., 1964.

Hansen describes the multi-track plan he helped develop in the high schools of Washington, D. C. On entrance to high school, a child is assigned to one of four tracks on the basis of various measures of his ability and achievement. Once assigned to a track, he takes most of his courses in that track, although there are some exceptions to this. A child is moved to a different track if his achievement indicates this is advisable.

The basic features of this plan are similar to that of "streaming" in English elementary schools (see book by Brian Jackson, following). Hansen's program is decidedly different from the plan at Melbourne High School (see book by B. Frank Brown, *The*

*Nongraded High School).* Hansen discusses many of the arguments for and against ability grouping. He also discusses problems associated with marking and the granting of diplomas. Chapters one, two, three, four and ten are especially interesting.

Jackson, Brian, *Streaming.* London: Routledge and Kegan Paul, 1964.

Streaming is the English equivalent of a multi-track plan in which elementary children of a given age are assigned to classrooms on the basis of achievement. There are usually three tracks: fast, average, and slow. The children assigned to one track remain there for all of their work. Children in a given classroom are taught by the whole-class method. There is a different curriculum for each track.

Chapter One of the present text indicates that there are three principal ways to implement a nongraded program. Streaming is illustrative of the second way. Children are assigned to classrooms according to performance levels. Streaming is practiced in the majority of English elementary schools. Its purpose is to provide for children's individual differences. Jackson questions the practice of streaming and suggests that schools where there are mixed achievement levels in classes may be more desirable.

# INDEX